25 WALKS

IN AND AROUND BELFAST

Paddy Dillon

Series Editor: Roger Smith

Northern Ireland
Tourist Board

EDINBURGH: The Stationery Office

First published 1996

Applications for reproduction should be made to The Stationery Office

Acknowledgements

The Publisher acknowledge with thanks the assistance and advice provided by local Councils and the Northern Ireland Tourist Board, who also supplied the photograph used on the front cover.

Thanks are also due to the author for providing the photographs used throughout the book.

British Library Cataloguing in Publication Data

A catalogue record for this book is available from the British Library

ISBN 0 11 495761 4

CONTENTS

USEFUL INFORMATION

The length of each walk is given in kilometres and miles, but within the text the measurements are metric for simplicity. The walks are described in detail and are supported by accompanying maps (study them before you start the walk), so there is little likelihood of getting lost, but if you want a back-up you will find the Ordnance Survey 1:50,000 Discoverer maps on sale locally, as well as a few maps offering greater detail to selected areas.

Every care has been taken to make the descriptions and maps as accurate as possible, but the author and publishers can accept no responsibility for errors, however caused. The countryside is always changing and there will inevitably be alterations to some aspects of these walks as time goes by. The publishers would be happy to receive comments and suggested alterations for future editions of the book.

General Information

Northern Ireland Tourist Board, 59 North Street, Belfast BT1 1NB (01232 246609). Open Mon-Sat 0900–1715, Sun (Jul-Aug) 1000–1600. General visitor information, accommodation advice and booking service. Bureau de Change. Starting point for a number of guided walks around Belfast city centre.

Other Tourist Information Centres are located at Belfast City and International Airports, Lisburn, Carrickfergus and Bangor. There are also a number of small tourist information points which generally stock a few leaflets relevant to an area, but do not handle accommodation bookings, etc.

The Environment Service manages a number of Country Parks around Belfast, including Scrabo, Redburn and Crawfordsburn Country Parks. Cave Hill Country Park, however, and most of the parks around the city of Belfast, are managed by the Belfast Parks Department. The Lagan Valley Regional Park is managed from an office in Belvoir Park Forest, and there are plans to establish a Belfast Hills Regional

METRIC MEASUREMENTS

At the beginning of each walk, the distance is given in miles and kilometres. Within the text, all measurements are metric for simplicity (and indeed our Ordnance Survey maps are now all metric). However, it was felt that a conversion table might be useful to those readers who still tend to think in terms of miles.

The basic statistic to remember is that one kilometre is five-eighths of a mile. Half a mile is equivalent to 800 metres and a quarter-mile is 400 metres. Below that distance, yards and metres are little different in practical terms.

km	miles
1	0.625
1.6	1
2	1.25
3	1.875
3.2	2
4	2.5
4.8	3
5	3.125
6	3.75
6.4	4
7	4.375
8	5
9	5.625
10	6.25
16	10

Park in future. The National Trust, Royal Society for the Protection of Birds, Conservation Volunteers and other groups have a specific interest in the management of some of the areas covered by these walks. Relevant telephone numbers are given in the information section to each walk.

A useful leaflet has been prepared by the Environment Service entitled 'Enjoying the Northern Ireland Countryside'. Access to the countryside is based on the provisions of the Access to the Countryside (Northern Ireland) Order 1983, and the leaflet summarises everyone's rights and responsibilities while walking in the countryside. There are moves to increase the amount of public access to the countryside throughout Northern Ireland.

Public Transport

It may come as a surprise to many readers to discover that there are privately operated bus companies which are reliable, frequent, reasonably priced and still able to make a profit without the need for vast subsidies. The Citybus and Ulsterbus services in and around Belfast are probably better for reaching the start of most of these walks than travelling by car. All you need to remember is that the red Citybus services operate only within the built-up parts of Belfast, while the blue Ulsterbus services operate to the fringes of the city and beyond, into the countryside.

To obtain timetable information, either call at the Citybus kiosk near the City Hall, or at the Ulsterbus stations at the Europa Bus Centre or Oxford Street. Citybus Timetable Enquiries, 01232 246485. Ulsterbus Timetable Enquiries, 01232 333000. There are tickets available which allow you to travel all day, all week, or longer, offering progressively better value for money. All the walks in this book were researched using Citybus and Ulsterbus services.

Northern Ireland Railways services could prove useful along both sides of Belfast Lough and through the Lagan Valley. Timetable information can be obtained from Belfast Central Station, or on 01232 230310.

Maps

The maps in this book should be sufficient for following each of the routes. However, the Ordnance Survey of Northern Ireland publishes a range of useful maps which you may also wish to use. The Greater Belfast Street Map is ideal for wandering around the city. Drawn at a scale of 1:12,000, it shows practically every street and bus route, as well as parks and prominent buildings. Discoverer Sheet 15 covers most of the walks in the book, while Discoverer Sheet 20 covers the remainder – both at a scale of 1:50,000. There are detailed maps of Scrabo and

Crawfordsburn Country Parks at scales of 1:4,000 and 1:5,000 respectively. The Street Map of Holywood and Bangor, at 1:10,000, proves useful on the North Down Coastal Path. Many popular sites have information boards showing the layouts of waymarked walks. Look out for them near entrance gates or car parks.

ACCESS TO THE COUNTRYSIDE IN NORTHERN IRELAND

Access issues are exhaustively covered under the provisions of the "Access to the Countryside (Northern Ireland) Order 1983". The Order is of course drafted in rather dry legal language, but the Environment Service have issued a more cheerfully worded leaflet entitled "Enjoying the Northern Ireland Countryside". It is recommended that walkers obtain a copy of this leaflet, which indicates other access opportunities beyond Belfast. There are probably more people walking in and around Belfast than in any other part of Northern Ireland, and there seem to be few areas where there is conflict over public access. However, all the land is owned by someone, and your passage across it is not necessarily of right.

City parks may have specific opening and closing times, and these are usually displayed at the entry points. More importantly, if you are using a car, you must retrieve it before the car park closes. Many of the walks in this book are not along routes which have been formally designated as rights of way, but are more properly referred to as "permitted paths". Even a waymarked walk or nature trail may not necessarily follow a right of way. Generally, the majority of these walks will be available to walkers practically all of the time.

Dogs can be taken on these walks, but they must always be kept under close control, and preferably on a lead whenever farmland is being crossed. Dogs should not be allowed to foul a path, cause a nuisance to other countryside users, or chase or worry livestock. If a sign specifically excludes dogs for any reason, then choose another walk.

Trespass occurs when you are crossing land without the consent of the landowner, following a route which is not a right of way or "permitted path". If you are caught trespassing you can be asked to leave the land, either directly to a public road, or by some other agreed and practicable route. You must be allowed to leave freely, although reasonable force could be used against you if you refuse to leave.

Most District Councils possess maps which show "alleged" rights of way, but so far, few District Councils have made any serious moves to formally dedicate rights of way, or have them signposted as such. This does, leave the walking public in a quandary, but the routes in this guidebook follow paths which are already being well used by walkers.

INTRODUCTION

The walks in this book are found in and around the city of Belfast. If you don't know the area, prepare to discover some delightfully varied walking country. Belfast is thrice blessed as it is situated within easy reach of the rugged slopes of the Belfast Hills, the rocky coastline of Belfast Lough, and the gentle countryside of the Lagan Valley. Even within the city there are pleasant public parks and interesting historical features to discover.

The first few walks are well within the city, exploring its heritage and parklands. You can either walk by yourself, or join a growing number of guided heritage walks and pub walks. For walks within the city, car parks are suggested, but you will also find that frequent Citybus services reach all the walks. If you want to discover the heritage of Belfast, then you will have to pound the pavements and search the streets to find it. Most of the walks in this book seek out the green spaces and open views.

Moving to the fringes of Belfast, there are a series of walks in the Lagan Valley Regional Park. These feature the River Lagan and the disused Lagan Canal. There is a continuous towpath walk from Belfast to Lisburn, as well as short circular walks around the Lagan Meadows, Giant's Ring, Belvoir Park Forest and Barnett Demesne. As you move further away from the city, it is more likely that you will need to use Ulsterbus services rather than Citybus services.

A series of walks explore the Belfast Hills. Apart from Cave Hill, this range of hills is relatively unfrequented. Approaches to the hills can be made from Colin Glen, Hannahstown, Carr's Glen, Belfast Castle or Belfast Zoo. In clear weather views extend over much of Northern Ireland and across the sea to Scotland. It is likely that a Belfast Hills Regional Park will be created in the future, which should enhance access opportunities to these rugged uplands. When venturing into the hills, it is advisable to use the Ordnance Survey of Northern Ireland Discoverer Sheet 15, which covers the whole area, should you go astray at any point.

The Belfast Hills gradually dwindle in stature, and there are a few other short walks on lower hills around Newtownabbey, Carrickfergus and Whitehead. Carrickfergus can with justification claim to be much older than Belfast, and has an Elizabethan parish church, a castle and recently uncovered town walls. A visit is recommended, although walking is largely restricted to a town trail and a tour of visitor and museum sites. Beyond Whitehead, there is a walk around Black Head, a rocky headland at the mouth of Belfast Lough.

Good coastal walks are generally a feature of the opposite side of Belfast Lough. The North Down Coastal Path could be sampled in its entirety, or you could complete shorter sections and explore inland too. There are walks around Bangor and Groomsport, at Crawfordsburn Country Park, or around Helen's Bay and Holywood. Each of these walks features access to the shore of Belfast Lough, and the route descriptions should enable you to complete the whole of the North Down Coastal Path from Holywood to Groomsport if you wish to enjoy a longer walk.

Newtownards is a fine little town not far from Belfast, and there are a few short walks worth savouring in the surrounding countryside. Scrabo Tower dominates the area, while Helen's Tower is less prominent. Both towers can be visited on short, varied walks where woodlands and open views are featured. Mount Stewart and its amazing gardens are also easily visited while in the area. Hillsborough is very much out on a limb, but as the village is close to the main Belfast to Dublin road, it is easily visited from Belfast and so is included in the book. You will need to use Ulsterbus services to access all the walks outside Belfast.

The 25 walks included here are mostly quite well trodden and may be cared for by the Belfast Parks Department, the Department for the Environment, or the local District Councils. Some areas may feature works which have been completed by bodies such as the Conservation Volunteers, or they may have been tidied and improved as part of an ACE scheme. ACE means 'Action for Community Employment' and projects give employment to workers from both sides of the community.

A running theme throughout most of these walks is the Ulster Way. This is essentially a long distance walking trail of some 977 km (570 miles) which completely encircles Northern Ireland. A wide loop of this walk encircles Belfast, taking in the North Down Coastal Path, the Lagan Canal Towpath and the Belfast Hills. If you were to follow the Ulster Way northwards you would be led through the Antrim Mountains, while if you followed it south along the shores of Strangford Lough you would eventually reach the Mountains of Mourne. Further west, in Fermanagh, it has links with other waymarked trails across the Border in the Republic of Ireland.

Practically all of these walks can be reached using public transport, and most of them have some place of refreshment nearby, if not actually on the route. You could dine in the splendour of Belfast Castle, or in one of a number of visitor centres, or simply at the pub or cafe down the road. There may be features of interest worth visiting, and where appropriate a note of the opening hours is supplied. It is advisable to check these in advance, as they are subject to change from time to time.

The walks are all fairly easy, and most of them are so well surfaced that comfortable shoes would be quite sufficient on a dry day. Most of the walks could easily be enjoyed by families with children. In some areas, however, there may be muddy patches, or the grass could be wet after a spell of rain, and boots would be more appropriate. In any case, you will need to dress for the weather whenever you venture outdoors. If you take a dog with you, please keep it under control, and note that there are bye-laws against the fouling of most public places.

While researching the routes for this book I have revisited many delightful places in and around Belfast. When I first explored around the city the walks I covered were quite long, but over the years I have been intrigued to find plenty of short and interesting walks tucked away in the most unlikely corners. I have also been thankful to find one or two derelict sites transformed into green areas with yet more walking potential. As Belfast embarks on more peaceful times, I would wish walkers who visit the city to take the time to explore and enjoy it as much as possible.

PADDY DILLON

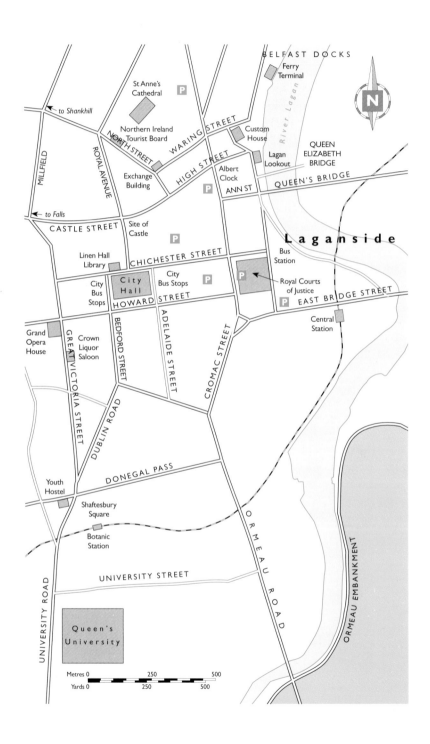

BELFAST CITY HERITAGE

Where to start – and what to see? Belfast has had an image flashed around the world's TV screens for many years which was always rather misleading. This is actually quite a young city which has grown from little more than a fishing village into an important industrial centre before suffering as much from recessions and depressions as from sectarianism and terrorism. The old city is largely buried beneath the new, and it is as well to start with what used to be there, before looking at the latest developments.

This is not an actual walking tour, but rather a series of suggestions of things you might want to see. You could spend a week or more pounding the city streets, following particular themes, or simply exploring every nook and cranny. There are specific guided walks and pub walks, as well as bus tours. Some of the later walks in this book are largely confined to the city in any case, so you can explore ever outwards from the centre.

Belfast grew from the confluence of the River Farset with the River Lagan, but the Farset now runs underground and cannot be seen. If you walk along High Street, you will be tracing its course. Other streets which can claim some antiquity include Ann Street, Waring Street, Bridge Street, North Street and Royal Avenue. Placenames in the city centre such as Castle Place, Castle Street, Castle Lane and Castlecourt all recall the castle and

City Hall, in the centre of Belfast.

INFORMATION

Distance: Variable.

Start and finish: City Hall, Tourist Information Centre, or any other prominent places.

Terrain: City streets and pavements, for which shoes are quite sufficient.

Public transport: Citybus services run to all parts of Belfast from stops within easy reach of the City Hall.

Time: Allow as long as you like to see as much as you want.

Refreshments: Plenty of places to eat and drink throughout the city centre and suburbs. There are even the Belfast Pub Walking Tours to consider!

Opening hours: *City Hall:* Wed 1030, must be booked in advance. Admission free (01232 320202). *Lagan Lookout Centre:* Mar-Sep, Mon-Fri, 1100–1700, Sat, 1200–1700, Sun, 1400–1700. Oct-Feb, Mon-Fri, 1130– 1530, Sat, 1300–1630, Sun, 1400–1630. Admission charge. For details of guided walks around the city, Pub Walking Tours, or Citybus Tours, contact the Tourist Information Centre, 59 North Street, Belfast (01232 246609).

castle grounds established by Sir Arthur Chichester, who obtained a Royal Charter for Belfast in 1613. The Chichesters eventually became the Earls of Donegall and practically ruled the early town of Belfast.

There is in fact nothing to see of old Belfast. The Long Bridge which spanned the River Lagan was completed in 1682, and was crossed by Schomberg and his troops in 1690. It was rebuilt and renamed Queen's Bridge in 1843. The castle was burnt down in 1708 and the Donegals moved to England for a while. Returning to Belfast, the family had a couple of fine houses before building Belfast Castle on the slopes of Cave Hill.

The leaning Albert Clock, Belfast.

In fact, the oldest building to be seen within the city of Belfast is the 1769 Exchange Building on the corner of Waring Street and Donegall Street, which in 1776 had the Assembly Rooms built on top. It is now a bank. It was in the middle of the 19th century that Belfast really began to develop. The Marquess of Donegall had to sell much of his property to pay off accrued debts, and speculators seized what they could and began to build a rather ramshackle city. Charles Lanyon, however, took a more long-term view and created much more solid buildings and institutions. Eventually, Lanyon became Mayor of Belfast, and his influence is found in places such as Queen's University, the Custom House, bridges, and many banks and churches.

Belfast's industries have included things as diverse as linen, shipbuilding and aircraft manufacture. It was the city where Dunlop experimented with pneumatic rubber tyres, and where Ferguson had a workshop before developing the world's most popular make of tractor. Buildings clustered around the City Hall have a distinctly 'Scottish commercial' look about them, and Belfast's population was drawn from many parts of Ireland, Scotland and England.

Sadly, the population was deeply divided on religious grounds, and unfortunately the different groups settled in different areas to produce ghettos. Friction in social circles and in employment and housing led eventually to civil disturbances, troops on the street and terrorism. Oddly enough, the ghetto areas themselves became places to visit as huge, colourful, political gable-end murals began to appear.

At one point the social night-life of Belfast was extremely limited, but for the past few years it has been quite vibrant. The Grand Opera House is easily reached from the City Hall, and there are a host of quaint pubs worth visiting. Pre-eminent is probably the Crown Liquor Saloon – a gas-lit establishment owned by the National Trust. Others nearby include Robinsons and Lavery's Gin Palace. A trio of very old pubs include White's Tavern dating from 1630, Kelly's Cellars from 1720 and Maddens at Smithfield.

In the gas-lit Crown Liquor Saloon.

The Empire contains bits and pieces from the SS Titanic, while Morrison's Spirit Grocers is in fact a recreation of a pub of yesteryear. Pubs which have some connection with Belfast's newspapers include The Duke of York and The Front Page. Bittles Bar is rather like an art gallery, while Magennis's, being near Belfast High Court, may feature barristers and solicitors at the bar. To learn more about these amazingly varied pubs, you are recommended to join one of the Belfast Pub Walking Tours.

After years of neglect, Belfast is rediscovering the River Lagan. The Laganside developments are stretching back from the Lagan Weir and the Lagan Lookout Centre to revamp the waterside. New walkways, new buildings and areas of greenery have already appeared, and there are interpretative panels which explain the history and heritage of the riverside. Elsewhere, the city is continually expanding into the countryside, and up the flanks of the Belfast Hills. Fortunately, as you will discover, there are still plenty of open spaces featuring fine walks in and around the city.

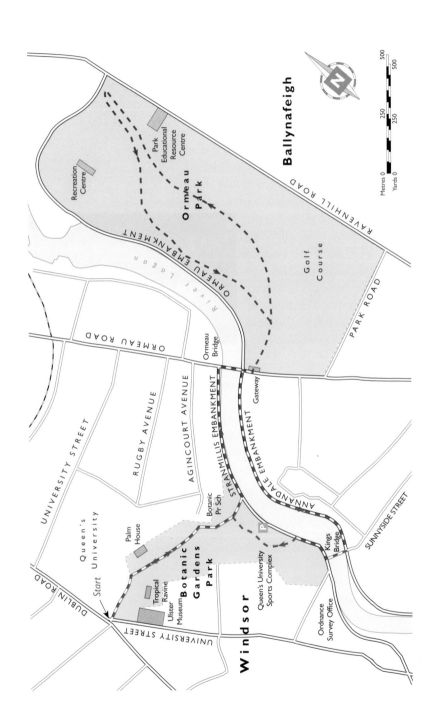

BOTANIC GARDENS AND ORMEAU PARK

The start of this walk is on three Citybus routes. If you prefer to arrive by car, you will need to use a small car park beside Stranmillis Embankment, and rather than walking through the main ornamental gateway into the Botanic Gardens, you arrive by way of a smaller back gate.

Prepare to be distracted right from the start of this walk. The entrance to the Botanic Gardens is between Queen's University and the Ulster Museum. You may be content to look at Queen's from afar, but a visit to the Ulster Museum is highly recommended. You can get a good grounding in the geology, flora and fauna of Ireland, as well as studying the history of Irish linen, or enquiring into the development of the city of Belfast.

When you emerge from the museum, there are two structures you should visit in the Botanic Gardens – the Palm House and the Tropical Ravine. The Palm House was founded in 1839 and had its distinctive dome added in 1852. It gradually fell into poor repair, but was completely renovated and reopened in 1983.

The Palm House, Botanic Gardens.

INFORMATION

Distance: 5 km (3 miles) if you visit both the gardens and the park.

Start and finish: At the gates of the Botanic Gardens, near the junctions of University Road, Malone Road and Stranmillis Road.

Terrain: Both the Botanic Gardens and Ormeau Park feature networks of clear, firm, dry tarmac paths, and short stretches of riverside roads are used to link both areas. No special footwear needed.

Public transport: Citybus services 69, 70 and 71 pass the Botanic Gardens, while Citybus services 38, 84, 85 and 87 cross Ormeau Bridge.

Time: As a walk, allow about 2 hours, but as there are so many important distractions, you might allow all day!

Refreshments: There are shops, pubs and restaurants within easy reach of this walk.

Opening hours: The Botanic Gardens and Ormeau Park close daily at dusk. The Palm House and Tropical Ravine are open Apr–Sep, Mon–Fri, 1000–1700, Sat, Sun and Bank Holidays, 1400–1700. Oct–Mar, Mon–Fri, 1000–1600, Sat, Sun and Bank Holidays, 1400–1600. Admission free (01232 324902). The Ulster Museum is open Mon–Fri, 1000–1700, Sat, 1300–1700, Sun, 1400–1700. Admission free (01232 381251).

Apart from a bewildering number of palms, you will find many exotic flowers and a section containing some gruesome insectivorous plants.

The warm and humid environment of the Palm House should prepare you for the hot and stifling atmosphere of the Tropical Ravine. This was founded in 1887, and like the Palm House was completely renovated and reopened in 1983. As you push through the exotic jungle in this hothouse, you almost expect to come face to face with a tiger, but there is nothing more ferocious than a pool full of turtles!

No matter how hot the weather may be, you will feel distinctly cool as you leave the Tropical Ravine. Walk down through the Botanic Gardens, noting the colourful flower beds and variety of trees. Go through a small, lower gateway and bear left to reach a children's play area near a car park. Cross the road and turn left to follow Stranmillis Embankment alongside the River Lagan. Cross the Ormeau Bridge, then pass through a large, stone-arched gateway into Ormeau Park.

Entrance gate to Ormeau Park.

This was originally the site of Ormeau Cottage, where the Donegall family moved in 1807. The area changed hands a couple of times before being earmarked as a potential site for a public park. In fact, this was Belfast's first municipal park – declared open in 1871 – and its layout is still largely based on Timothy Hervey's original landscaping.

You can wander at will through the park using a variety of paths, but there are two fairly clear paths which allow you to walk the length of the park and back again. As you enter the park, follow the most broad and obvious path gently uphill. This path passes wooded areas, flower beds, benches and shelters, running close to a golf course for a while. Keep to this path until you almost leave the park at another gateway.

Don't leave the park, but turn sharply left before the gateway, and pass close to a large sports complex. Keep to the left of a series of sports fields to follow a path uphill a short way. You will find yourself passing through wooded areas overlooking the Ormeau Embankment and the city. Simply follow the path onwards until you eventually join the broader path leading back towards the gateway used earlier to enter the park.

Looking to the city from Ormeau Park.

When you leave the park, cross Ormeau Road, but don't cross the Ormeau Bridge. Instead, walk alongside the River Lagan using the Annadale Embankment, passing Dunne's Stores on the way to King's Bridge. The large building you see above the trees beyond King's Bridge is Colby House – the headquarters of the Ordnance Survey of Northern Ireland. Cross King's Bridge and turn right along the Stranmillis Embankment. A small gateway reveals a path which runs back towards the Botanic Gardens, and you can explore this amazing area for a second time if you wish.

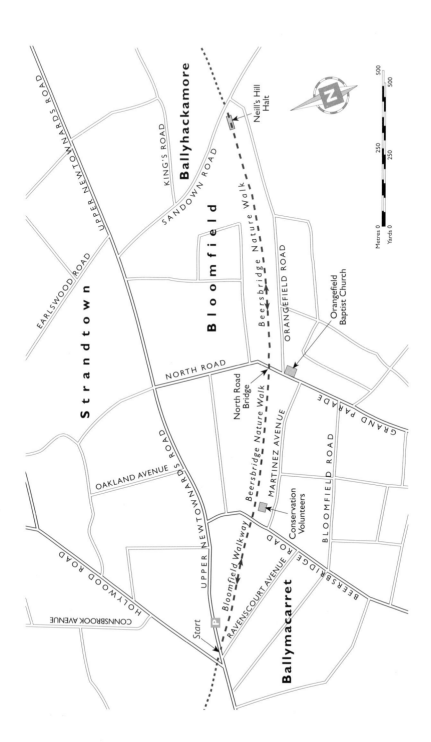

BEERSBRIDGE NATURE WALK

The Bloomfield Walkway and Beersbridge Nature Walk are based on the same railway trackbed in East Belfast. Trains ran for just a century – from 1850 to 1950 – along a line which stretched from Belfast Docks to Comber, Donaghadee and Newcastle. After closure, the line was neglected and became overgrown in places. Some parts were used for dumping rubbish.

The Bloomfield Walkway in East Belfast.

The trackbed has been developed as an amenity in two stages. The Bloomfield Walkway is maintained by Belfast Parks Department, and features a path running through areas of trimmed grass. The Beersbridge Nature Walk is maintained by the Conservation Volunteers and is an altogether wilder sort of trail. You can compare and contrast both short walks, and you can either walk them both twice as a there-and-back route, or walk one-way and use a Citybus service to leave the far end.

INFORMATION

Distance: 5 km (3 miles) walking there-and-back.

Start and finish: On the A20 at the junctions of Newtownards Road, Upper Newtownards Road and Holywood Road in East Belfast.

Terrain: Level, firm, dry, well-surfaced paths, for which ordinary shoes are usually sufficient.

Public transport: Numerous buses serve the start of the walk, including Citybus services 20 to 27, 76 and 77. Citybus services 24, 76 and 77 operate along Sandown Road at the end of the walk.

Time: Allow 2 hours for the walk there-and-back, or one hour if you walk the route one-way and return by bus.

Refreshments: There are pubs, shops and cafes close to the start of the walk where the three roads intersect.

Opening hours: The Bloomfield Walkway and Beersbridge Nature Walk are always open and admission is free. The Conservation Volunteers base is open normal working hours.

Start at the point where Newtownards Road becomes Upper Newtownards Road, and where Holywood Road branches away from both of them. You actually start just on Holywood Road, close to a carpet shop. There is a small car park behind the carpet shop, if you arrive by car, and a large plaque built into a wall points out that you are on the Bloomfield Walkway.

Simply follow the path, which runs between areas of short green grass. Looking forward, there is no doubt where you should be heading. To the left and right, rows of terraced houses flank the old trackbed, where once the inhabitants would have heard trains rattling past. Looking back, you can see the two huge, yellow shipyard cranes at Harland & Wolff – nicknamed Samson and Goliath. The Bloomfield Walkway ends suddenly at the next road, which is Beersbridge Road. Cross the road to reach the start of the Beersbridge Nature Walk.

The Beersbridge Nature Walk.

You are immediately hemmed in by hedging and shrubbery as you follow a narrow path along the old trackbed, but the surroundings become more spacious after a short while. There may be a few Conservation Volunteers on duty at a workbase in a fenced compound, and they would gladly tell you what is currently worth seeing as you proceed through the cutting.

Have a look at the raised gardens which are tended by wheelchair users, planted with fragrant herbs which can be appreciated by people from the nearby Blind

Centre for Northern Ireland. It is hoped that tactile maps and interpretative facilities will eventually be made available for blind people to use on this walk.

As you follow the path onwards, there is a Butterfly Bank on the left, where a dozen species have been noted throughout the summer months. There are plenty of trees, bushes and flowers to observe as the seasons change, and the area has been kept deliberately wild so that insects, mammals and birds can forage for food and have safe areas away from human interference. Small ponds have been created to offer a more varied range of habitats.

The nature walk goes under North Road, where the original arch has had to be strengthened to carry an extra load of traffic. Once you have passed under the bridge and walked a little further along the trackbed, look back over your shoulder and you will see the Orangefield Baptist Church. This is very much part of the city, and yet from the nature walk it looks more like a little country chapel.

The former Neill's Hill Halt can be spotted if you look for the old platforms at the side of the trackbed. It was opened in 1890 and had a subway to link the two platforms. You suddenly emerge on Sandown Road, and you wouldn't be able to continue much further at present, although more of the old trackbed may be made available for quiet recreation in the future.

There is a bus stop immediately available on Sandown Road, or you could turn around and walk all the way back to the start and enjoy everything all over again. The Beersbridge Nature Walk is a popular choice for school groups, and is proving to be a useful educational resource in such a built-up part of the city.

The Beersbridge Nature Walk.

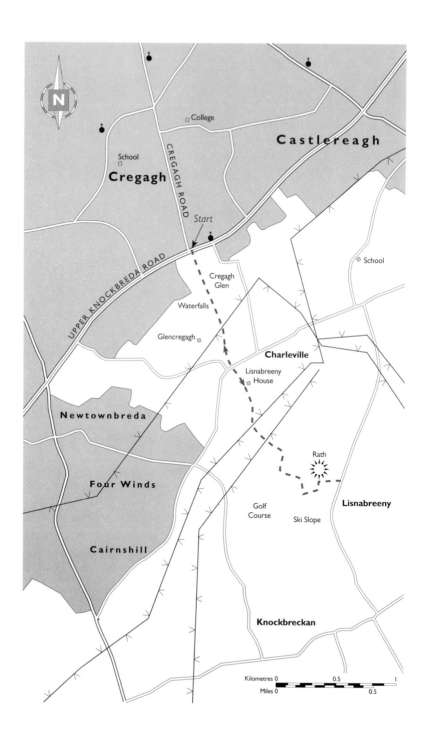

CREGAGH GLEN AND LISNABREENY

Cregagh Glen is heralded by a large wooden sign between two stone towers beside the busy dual-carriageway Upper Knockbreda Road, close to the point where Cregagh Road joins it. The glen is owned and managed by the National Trust, and the long distance Ulster Way runs through

it. Well-wooded and steep-sided, the nature of the glen focusses the walker's attention to nearby details. The Ulster Way can be followed higher into the fields above the glen, where views stretch all the way across Belfast, Belfast Lough and the Belfast Hills.

The entrance to Cregagh Glen.

Citybus services run past the entrance to Cregagh Glen, but if you walk to the top of the glen, or even higher to Lisnabreeny, then there are no other bus services. There is a small roadside car park at Lisnabreeny if you can arrange for someone to collect you, otherwise you will have to walk all the way back down through Cregagh Glen again. There is no handy place to park a car near the entrance to the glen, the only alternative being on-street parking away from the busy Upper Knockbreda Road.

Pass through the entrance to Cregagh Glen and note how suddenly the scene changes from a busy dual-carriageway road to a quiet and well-wooded glen. There is a firm path, several footbridges, and many flights of steps running up through the glen not too far from the course of the little river which it contains.

INFORMATION

Distance: 5 km (3 miles) if walked both ways.

Start and finish: At Cregagh, opposite the junction of Cregagh Road and Upper Knockbreda Road.

Terrain: Cregagh Glen is well-wooded, featuring made-up paths and flights of steps, and there are also gravel and grassy paths on the way uphill to Lisnabreeny. Boots are recommended, particularly in wet weather.

Public transport: Citybus services 31 and 33 run along Upper Knockbreda Road, and Citybus services 34, 78 and 85 terminate quite close to the junction of both roads.

Time: Allow about 2 hours if walking both ways.

Refreshments: Nothing actually along the way, but plenty of places to eat and drink back towards the city.

The glen is pleasantly wooded and features a good covering of ferns and mosses, with abundant flowers in early summer. There is a fine little waterfall, which is best visited after heavy rain, when it puts on a more impressive display.

As you climb up through the glen, there are a couple of paths leading away from the river. Two of these paths climb flights of steps to reach viewpoints, while towards the top of the glen, a path on the left simply runs at a slightly higher elevation than the riverside path. If you climb up either of the viewpoint paths, you must descend afterwards to continue walking up along the main path. When you leave the glen, a

Well constructed path in Cregagh Glen.

path runs through a tunnel beneath the minor Manse Road, and a wooden walkway has been installed inside the tunnel. You could turn back at this point, or continue uphill following the Ulster Way to Lisnabreeny.

Emerging from the tunnel, follow a path uphill to the left, then turn right to walk along a gravel track which passes Lisnabreeny House. This track quickly leaves the woodlands near Lisnabreeny House and reaches a hillside close to a golf course. When you reach the end of the track, turn left and walk uphill, on ground which can be muddy, then turn right to trace the top edge of the golf course. Looking back over your shoulder, you can see the city spreading away towards the Belfast Hills and Belfast Lough. Turning left around the edge of a high field, you reach a stand of trees which encircles the hilltop rath at Lisnabreeny.

The earthern ramparts of the rath are very easily distinguished and display the classic circular form. There are countless numbers of raths across the face of Ireland, and these are peculiarly Irish features of the landscape. They were basically fortified farmsteads occupied by fairly prosperous extended family groups in early Christian times. The circular earthern rampart would once have had a palisade fence around its rim, and there would have been post and wattle huts within the enclosure.

For many centuries it was considered to be unlucky to level the ramparts or attempt to bring the land inside a rath into cultivation. Raths have been believed to be the abode of the Fairy folk, and so have been largely left untouched. Raths are often readily distinguished in open fields by the unkempt trees or bushes

The tunnel leading onwards to Lisnabreeny.

which grow from them. Fortunately, as the countryside superstitions associated with such sites began to wane, the desire to conserve these places purely for their heritage value has increased.

There is a fenced pathway leading away from the rath at Lisnabreeny, reaching a small parking space beside Lisnabreeny Road. This is as far as it is worth walking – the onward stretch of the Ulster Way is all road walking until it reaches Stormont, Redburn Country Park and the coastal path beyond Holywood. If you can arrange to be collected by car at Lisnabreeny, the walk can end there, otherwise you must retrace your steps back through Cregagh Glen to reach the bus services far below on either Cregagh Road or Upper Knockbreda Road. There are the views across the city and surrounding countryside to enjoy before you are swallowed into Cregagh Glen on the descent.

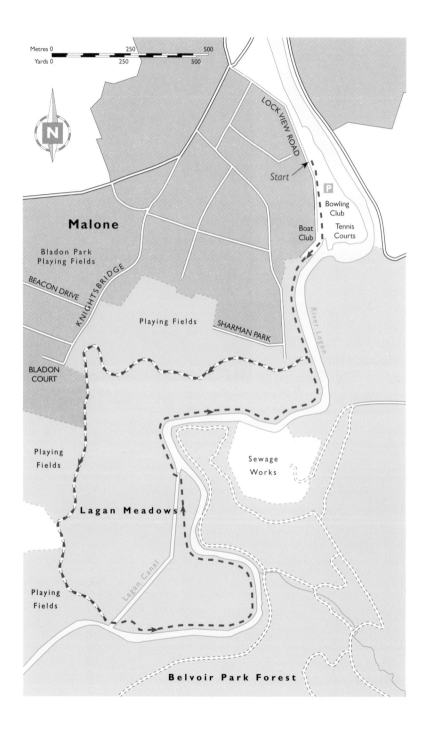

LAGAN MEADOWS

There are many paths and tracks through the Lagan Valley Regional Park, and on this short walk the Lagan Meadows are explored. This is the part of the Regional Park which lies closest to the city, with easy access from Stranmillis, and yet it still boasts open grasslands and wooded areas. In addition, there is easy access across the River Lagan to Belvoir Park Forest, and as the suggested route includes a stretch of the Lagan Canal Towpath, there are obvious extensions along the valley either back towards the centre of Belfast or away to Lisburn.

The Cutters Wharf beside the River Lagan.

There is a car park on Lockview Road, just beyond the Cutters Wharf riverside restaurant. You can get close to this point using Citybus services, then walk along Lockview Road and continue through the car park. There is an information board towards the end of the car park, offering brief notes about the Lagan Canal Towpath and parts of the Lagan Valley Regional Park. From the noticeboard, a paved path leads through an area of shrubbery. After passing a rowing club and tennis courts, you follow the Lagan Canal Towpath alongside the River Lagan.

The Lagan Canal isn't a continuous cut, but a series of short canals by-passing any sudden changes in level along the River Lagan. The various stretches of the

INFORMATION

Distance: 6 km (4 miles).

Start and finish: At the car park beyond the Cutters Wharf, Lockview Road, Belfast.

Terrain: Mostly clear and obvious gravel tracks or grassy paths, for which boots are recommended in wet weather.

Public transport: Citybus service 69 runs past Lockview Road near the start of the walk.

Time: Allow 2–3 hours for the full circuit around the Lagan Meadows, although this walk can be shortened if required.

Refreshments: The only place offering immediate refreshments is the Cutters Wharf restaurant at the start of the walk, although there are many other places to eat and drink back towards the city.

Opening times: The Lagan Meadows are always open. Information about this and other parts of the Lagan Valley Regional Park from the Park Office (01232 491922).

canal were constructed from the 1760s until the 1790s – by which time the system was navigable from Belfast to Lisburn. Coal was perhaps the most important cargo moved along the canal, but the developing road and railway routes ultimately led to the demise of the navigation.

As you walk along the broad and obvious tarmac towpath beside the river, watch out for a turning off to the right, through a small gate, just next to a bench. A short path leads up towards the houses at the end of Sharman Road, where you go left through another gate and then right to follow a clear gravel path gently uphill. You walk fairly close to the houses built along Sharman Park, then head off to the left around the side of a playing field. Simply follow the clear path all the way up to a gate which leads onto Bladon Drive.

Don't go through this gate, but turn left and start following another clear gravel path gently downhill. The land downhill from the path is managed by the Ulster Wildlife Trust as a nature reserve, featuring open flowery grasslands and areas of trees and shrubs. Later, the path undulates along the top side of the Lagan Valley, with views towards the city before it runs through more wooded surroundings. Eventually, a long flight of steps leads straight down through the woods to land on the Lagan Canal Towpath again.

Lagan Meadows, managed as a nature reserve.

Bear slightly to the left and then right to cross a footbridge over a spur of the derelict Lagan Canal. Do not, however, cross the next footbridge over the River Lagan, which would lead you into Belvoir Park Forest. Turn left instead to cross a stile and follow the River Lagan downstream, walking around a broad loop of the river with a level meadow on your left and the mixed woodlands of Belvoir Park Forest rising on your right. A few mature oak trees stand in the riverside meadow, lending grace to the scene.

Later, you will find yourself walking along a broad strip of wooded land between the River Lagan and the derelict Lagan Canal. Towards the end of this strip you cross a footbridge on the left, which spans the old canal, then turn right to follow the Lagan Canal Towpath onwards. The tarmac towpath leads back downstream alongside the River Lagan, and eventually brings you back to the car park near the Cutters Wharf riverside restaurant, where refreshments are available.

An obvious extension to this walk would be to cross the footbridge over the River Lagan and enter Belvoir Park Forest to sample a number of short waymarked trails. If you were to proceed much further along the Lagan Canal Towpath, you would find that the Ulster Way was also routed along its middle stretches.

Walking in a wooded part of the Lagan Meadows.

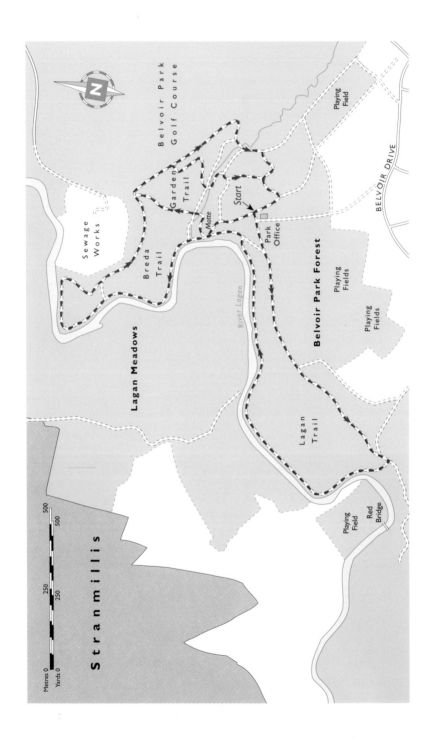

BELVOIR PARK FOREST

Belvoir (pronounced beaver) has a long history, and it is still possible to see a fine Norman motte close to the Forest Education Centre. The estate dates from Plantation times, and was first enclosed by the Hills of Hillsborough. It was Arthur Hill-Trevor who first settled there in the 18th century, and became the first Viscount Dungannon. His daughter Anne was the mother of the Duke of Wellington. After many more changes of ownership, Belvoir became a naval arms depot, before being opened as a public amenity in 1961.

The emphasis at Belvoir Park Forest is on education, and the forest is popular with visiting school groups. A large courtyard building is used as an education centre, and at certain times there is a small exhibition open to the public. There are various leaflets available explaining all about forestry, how to identify trees, as well as about the Lagan Valley Regional Park. The courtyard building houses the Lagan Valley Regional Park Office, as well as the RSPB Regional Office.

There are three colour-coded waymarked trails in the forest. As they are all quite short, they might as well be walked one after another. An information board beside the car park outlines the routes of the Lagan Trail, Breda Trail and Garden Trail – which are waymarked red, blue and yellow on stout wooden posts for easy route-finding. The waymarking system is so good that detailed route directions are hardly necessary. Looking out from the

Kingfisher sculpture in Belvoir Park Forest.

INFORMATION

Distance: Up to 4 km (2.5 miles) by combining a series of short waymarked trails.

Start and finish: Belvoir Park Forest Education Centre, near Belvoir in South Belfast.

Terrain: Mostly firm forest tracks and paths, but some parts can be a little muddy in wet weather, so boots are recommended.

Public transport: Ulsterbus services 13 and 25B run to Belvoir, close to the entrance to Belvoir Park Forest.

Time: Allow 1½ to 2 hours to cover all three of the short waymarked trails in the forest.

Refreshments: None within the forest, although there is a small shop just off Belvoir Drive on the way to the forest.

Opening hours: Belvoir Park Forest closes at dusk. The Forest Education Centre is occasionally open and admission is free (01232 491264). The Royal Society for the Protection of Birds (RSPB) Regional Office can be contacted on 01232 491547, and the Lagan Valley Regional Park Office on 01232 491922.

car park, there is a view across the Lagan Meadows and Lagan Valley to the Belfast Hills.

Starting from the car park beside the Forest Education Centre, there is a prominent wooden sculpture of a kingfisher, and a waymark post with a red arrow pointing leftwards indicates the start of the Lagan Trail. Follow the track which is indicated, running downhill through the forest, before proceeding along a level course for a while. After passing through a crossroads of tracks, the Lagan Trail climbs up to another crossroads of tracks.

Turn right and right again to follow a clear path down towards the River Lagan, then follow the river downstream. The path climbs, then descends, passing a footbridge before continuing downstream. Don't cross the footbridge, but note that it gives access to the Lagan Meadows. Eventually, the Lagan Trail climbs back up towards the car park. Just before reaching the car park, however, you can turn left and start following the Breda Trail, which is marked by blue arrows on waymark posts.

The Red Bridge crosing the River Lagan.

The Breda Trail runs downhill, up, and down again to follow the River Lagan further downstream. The path runs around a pronounced meander in the river, where young oaks have been planted, then climbs uphill to follow the forest boundary. If you look out from the trees, you will see Belvoir Park Golf Course. Follow the blue arrows faithfully and you will turn right to walk downhill beside the Big Wood Forest Nature Reserve. Cross a footbridge, climb over a hump, then cross another footbridge before climbing back up to the car park.

To follow the short Garden Trail, you should look out for yellow waymark arrows – aiming first for the prominent Norman motte just below the car park. The trail then runs down into a valley and crosses a bridge below an ivy-clad pipeline, before running up a flight of steps. The edge of the forest is reached, where you turn right, then right again as indicated by the next yellow arrow. The trees on this trail are planted more formally than elsewhere in the forest, and there are open areas of cropped grass.

Follow the yellow arrows faithfully, as you will be passing through a network of paths before climbing back up to the car park. On at least some part of each of these three trails, you will be following the course of the Ulster Way, which wanders through Belvoir Park Forest on its immense circuit around Northern Ireland. If you were to follow the Ulster Way in one direction you would reach Cregagh Glen, while in the other direction you would be drawn along the Lagan Canal Towpath.

Belvoir Park Forest and the River Lagan.

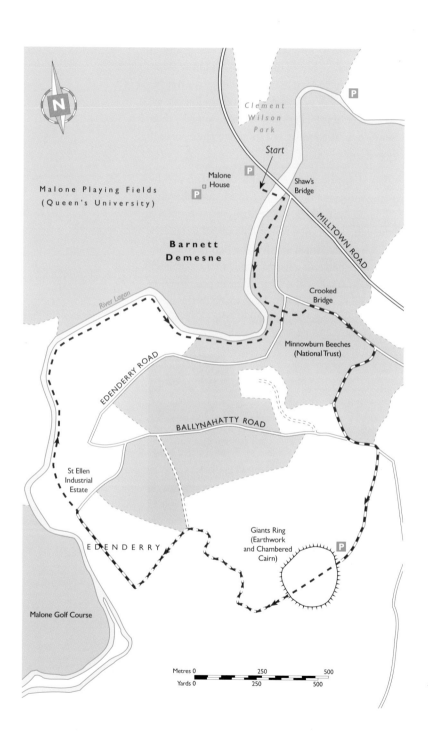

GIANT'S RING AND EDENDERRY

This circuit is short, but runs through a part of the Lagan Valley which is both varied and interesting. It includes features such as the fine old Shaw's Bridge, the stately Minnowburn Beeches, the prehistoric Giant's Ring, the former mill village of Edenderry and a lovely riverside path running beside the Lagan. From the higher ground there are splendid views across the Lagan Valley towards the Belfast Hills.

The walk starts at the car park beside Shaw's Bridge, where an information board offers a few background

The Minnowburn Beeches on a steep bank.

notes about this part of the Lagan Valley Regional Park. Cross over Shaw's Bridge, turning left to go down a flight of steps between the old stone-arched

INFORMATION

Distance: 6 km (4 miles), although there are paths which allow the walk to be shortened.

Start and finish: At the car park at Shaw's Bridge, off Milltown Road, between Malone and Belvoir in South Belfast.

Terrain: Mostly firm paths, but some parts can be muddy after rain, so boots are recommended.

Public transport: Ulsterbus service 13 runs close to Shaw's Bridge at the start of this walk.

Time: Allow 2–2½ hours for the circuit.

Refreshments: Nothing actually on the route, although there may be an ice-cream van parked at Shaw's Bridge, and the Barnett Restaurant is just off-route at Malone House.

bridge and the more modern concrete and steel span of the new road bridge. Turn left again to go underneath an arch of Shaw's Bridge and start following the wooded riverside path upstream.

The path follows the River Lagan only for a short way, then is diverted leftwards by the inflowing Purdy's Burn. Cross a minor road in view of the tall Minnowburn Beeches, which are planted on a steep bank and cared for by the National Trust. Continue following Purdy's Burn upstream to the next minor road and turn right to cross the Crooked Bridge, then follow road signs showing the way to the Giant's Ring. These will lead you off to the right up the Giant's Ring Road, then left, then right again to reach a small car park beside the Giant's Ring. There is an information board beside the car park which offers a few thoughts about the Giant's Ring and the surrounding area.

In the centre of the Giant's Ring.

The Giant's Ring is one of the most mysterious sites in the Lagan Valley Regional Park and its purpose, although obscure, was almost certainly ritualistic. The Giant's Ring is basically a 'henge' – featuring a circular earthwork embankment with a small, bouldery structure in the centre – and is reckoned to be around 4000 years old. Horse races were once held around the inside of the ring, while spectators lined the top of the embankment. From the embankment there are views across the Lagan Valley towards the Belfast Hills. You can either walk all the way around the embankment, or simply walk straight across the ring and follow a path leading away from the far side.

The narrow path leading away from the Giant's Ring is fenced and well-trodden, so you will have no difficulty following it through the fields. However, 600 m after leaving the Giant's Ring, you should take care to spot a turning off to the left, where a field path is at first obscured by gorse bushes but later descends straight towards the village of Edenderry. Go through a gateway on the right to enter the village, then walk straight through by road. Normally this village of terraced houses is quiet, but it is a popular venue for Orangemen on 12th July each year, when the main Belfast Orange Order parade ends in a large field close to the village. When you reach the St Ellen Industrial Estate, there is a small gate on the left, and a narrow tarmac path leads down to Gilchrist's Bridge which spans the River Lagan.

The former mill village of Edenderry.

Don't cross the bridge, which was named in honour of the first chairman of the Lagan Valley Regional Park, but follow the riverside path downstream. You will probably spot people walking or cycling along the path on the opposite side of the Lagan, which is the Lagan Canal Towpath. You pass a small, wooded, riverside nature reserve, which is managed by the Ulster Wildlife Trust. The path you are following stays faithful to the course of the River Lagan, except for a short detour to cross Purdy's Burn near the Minnowburn Beeches. From that point, it is simply a matter of retracing your earlier steps to return to Shaw's Bridge and end the walk.

Shaw's Bridge is actually the third bridge to span the River Lagan at this point. The first bridge was a temporary structure of oak built by Captain Shaw in 1655 to help get Cromwell's big guns across the river. This was a time of battles, massacres and population displacement, with many of the native Irish faring no better than the oaks which were felled to form the first bridge. A second bridge was swept away during a storm, and the present bridge was built in 1709.

This short circular walk is easily combined with other walks in the Lagan Valley Regional Park. The Lagan Canal Towpath can be followed either towards Belfast or Lisburn, or you could combine this short circular walk with the walk around Barnett Demesne and Dixon Park. You could also extend this walk slightly by walking underneath the modern road bridge and enjoying a short stroll through Clement Wilson Park.

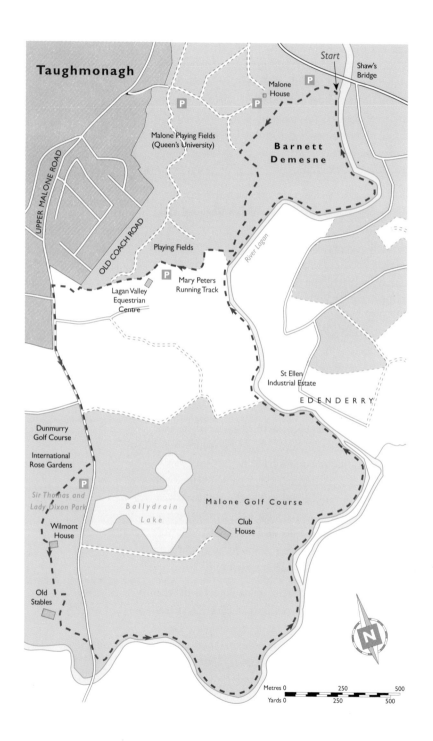

Taughmonagh

Start

Shaw's
Bridge

Malone
House

Barnett
Demesne

Malone Playing Fields
(Queen's University)

UPPER MALONE ROAD

OLD COACH ROAD

River Logan

Playing Fields

Mary Peters
Running Track

Lagan Valley
Equestrian
Centre

St Ellen
Industrial Estate

E D E N D E R R Y

Dunmurry
Golf Course

International
Rose Gardens

*Sir Thomas and
Lady Dixon Park*

*Ballydrain
Lake*

Malone Golf Course

Club
House

Wilmont
House

Old
Stables

N

Metres 0   250   500
Yards 0   250   500

BARNETT DEMESNE

The Lagan Valley was once filled with large estates, and this walk passes through the former Barnett Demesne, Ballydrain and Wilmont estates. It also passes the former mill village of Edenderry and takes in a good stretch of the Lagan Canal Towpath. Barnett Demesne and Wilmont are now public parks, with the Wilmont estate now being known as Sir Thomas and Lady Dixon Park – or Dixon Park for short.

The walk through this part of the Lagan Valley wanders from park to park, then returns via the Lagan Canal Towpath, and how much time you spend exploring the parks is entirely up to you. Shaw's Bridge is the starting point, although there are other car parks around the route. Ulsterbus services stop near Shaw's Bridge, while Citybus services stop near Malone House, for walkers who choose not to arrive by car.

INFORMATION

Distance: 9 km (5.5 miles), although there are paths allowing the walk to be shortened.

Start and finish: At the car park at Shaw's Bridge, off Milltown Road, between Malone and Belvoir in South Belfast.

Terrain: Mostly firm parkland paths and a towpath, but some woodland paths can be muddy after rain, and boots are recommended.

Public transport: Ulsterbus service 13 passes Shaw's Bridge, and Citybus service 71 passes Malone House just above Shaw's Bridge.

Time: Allow 3 or 4 hours, as there are plenty of things to see along the way.

Refreshments: There is sometimes an ice-cream van parked at Shaw's Bridge, with the Barnett Restaurant available at Malone House and The Stables Coffee House in Sir Thomas and Lady Dixon Park.

Opening hours: *Malone House:* open all year, Mon-Sat, 1000–1630, admission free (01232 681246). *Barnett Demesne:* always open. *Sir Thomas and Lady Dixon Park, including the International Rose Garden:* open daily until dusk, admission free.

Shaw's Bridge crosses the River Lagan.

Malone House in Barnett Demesne.

Starting at Shaw's Bridge, there is an information board giving a few background notes about this part of the Lagan Valley. Next to the board is a gateway and signpost; the latter indicates that the Lagan Canal Towpath is also used by the Ulster Way. Go through the gate, turn right and walk steeply uphill towards Malone House – a landmark property built in the 1820s on the site of an earlier fort. It was given to the city in 1946, destroyed by fire in 1976 and restored and reopened by 1983. There is a gallery, a series of elegant rooms, the Barnett Restaurant and an exhibition about the Belfast Parks.

Turn left to follow a tarmac footpath away from the house. This path is soon flanked by trees, and when the tarmac ends you turn left and walk downhill. Look out for a right turn, where a path leads into woodlands. Keep to the most obvious paths in the woods, drifting gradually downhill. You should later look out for a path running uphill to the right which emerges at the Mary Peters Track. This running track honours Mary's achievement in the 1972 Munich Olympics, where she gained a gold medal in the pentathlon.

Follow the access road uphill and away from the running track, then turn left along Old Coach Lane and the busy Upper Malone Road. Follow the road

Wilmont House in Dixon Park.

until you reach the entrance gates to Sir Thomas and Lady Dixon Park. There is a clear tarmac drive leading through the park towards Wilmont House, but off to the right is the City of Belfast International Rose Garden which is well worth seeing when it is in full bloom.

The Wilmont estate was presented to the City of Belfast in 1959 and is now commonly known as Dixon Park. The International Rose Garden was opened in 1990 and features elaborate landscaping, trial beds, information panels and up to 20,000 rose bushes blooming throughout the summer months. For rose aficionados, Rose Week is the third week in July each year.

Beyond Wilmont House is a children's play area, then The Stables Coffee House is passed before a path leads down to the Lagan Canal Towpath. Keep left to follow the old towpath underneath Drum Bridge. The Lagan Canal Towpath is followed all the way back to Shaw's Bridge, and this is a such a clear and obvious path that a detailed route description is hardly needed, but there are a few features to help you keep track of your progress.

Before long you will leave the actual riverside and walk alongside a stretch of disused canal, where you pass under an old footbridge. The towpath runs within sight of Malone Golf Course, and later passes a picnic site at the Eel Weir. The mill village of Edenderry, St Ellen Industrial Estate and Gilchrist's Bridge are all passed close together, on the opposite bank of the river. The towpath continues beside woodlands which are part of Barnett Demesne, leading back to Shaw's Bridge where the walk started.

Shaw's Bridge was built in 1709, replacing a structure which was washed away in a storm. The first bridge was of oak, built by Captain Shaw in 1655 to allow the Cromwelleans to get their big guns across the River Lagan. The present stone-arched bridge is no longer used by traffic, which now thunders across a nearby concrete and steel bridge.

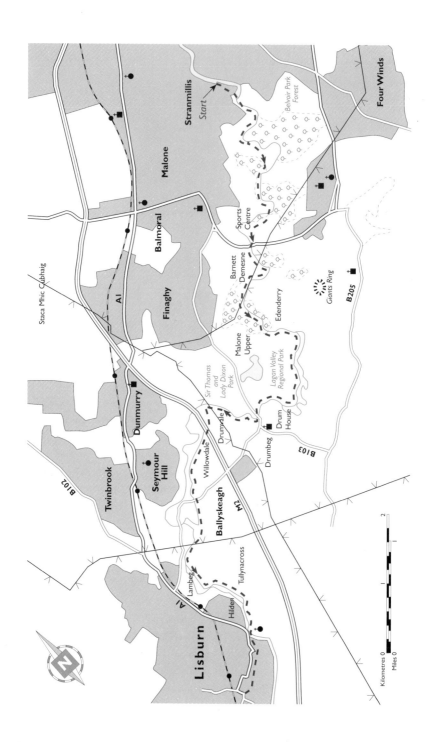

LAGAN CANAL TOWPATH

The Cutters Wharf on Lockview Road is a riverside restaurant beside the Lagan, and just beyond it is a large car park. Walk to the far end of the car park and you will find an information board showing the course of the Lagan Canal Towpath. It also shows other public access areas alongside the River Lagan, such as forests, parks and nature reserves.

Strange bent tree beside the River Lagan.

Leave the information board and follow a paved path through a shrubbery. You pass a rowing club and tennis courts before joining the Lagan Canal Towpath. The towpath is aligned to the River Lagan and you start to follow it upstream. The river banks are well-wooded, so you navigate mainly by bridges, ticking them off as you pass them.

As you turn a right-hand bend in the river, the open fields of the Lagan Meadows are nearby, while the opposite bank features the mixed woodlands of Belvoir Park Forest. A broad loop of the River Lagan has been severed by a short length of canal – complete with towpath. As you turn another loop of the River Lagan, you pass a golf driving range.

To stay on the course of the Lagan Canal Towpath, you should cross the Red Bridge over the River Lagan (3 km after the start of the walk), then cross a narrow, stone-arched bridge over another stretch of the old canal cutting. Turn right after crossing the bridge and continue beside the old cut, and you will soon be led back onto the banks of the River Lagan. At this point,

INFORMATION

Distance: 17 km (10.5 miles) as a linear walk.

Start and finish: Start on Lockview Road in Belfast and finish in the centre of Lisburn.

Terrain: The Lagan Canal Towpath is a firm, dry, tarmac path running beside either the River Lagan or a series of derelict canal spurs. No special footwear needed.

Public transport: Citybus service 69 passes Lockview Road near the start of the walk. Numerous Ulsterbus City Stopper services run from Lisburn to Belfast, as do Northern Ireland Railways.

Time: Allow 5 hours for the full walk, although it can be split at some of the bridges using Ulsterbus services.

Refreshments: Nothing along the way, although shops, pubs and cafes can be found a short way off-route. Lisburn, at the end of the walk, has plenty of places to eat and drink.

Opening hours: *Irish Linen Centre and Lisburn Museum:* Apr-Sep, Mon-Sat, 0900–1730, Sun, 1400–1730. Oct-Mar, Mon-Sat, 0930–1700, Sun, 1400–1700. Admission charge (01846 663377).

an elaborate system of weirs and chutes is used by canoeists.

A short walk upstream takes you under the arch of a busy, modern road bridge, immediately before you reach the mellow stone arches of the much older Shaw's Bridge. Climb up a flight of steps to the left, then turn right to cross Shaw's Bridge. You will reach a car park with an information board, signpost and gateway. The signpost indicates that you are following a stretch of the Ulster Way. As you proceed further upstream, you will have Barnett Demesne off to your right, while across the River Lagan are the lovely Minnowburn Beeches, cared for by the National Trust.

There are sports facilities off to the right above the Lagan, and you should notice the St Ellen Industrial Estate and the worker's village of Edenderry on the far bank. Gilchrist's Bridge – a stout footbridge – offers access to the village if required, but remember to come back across the footbridge to continue the walk. Further upstream, you will notice that the Lagan Canal Towpath is again routed alongside a canal cutting. You pass a picnic site at the Eel Weir, and Malone Golf Course is close to hand on the right; later, there are fields and occasional large houses to be seen. You will find yourself again following the banks of the River Lagan for a short while.

A road is reached at Drum Bridge, but there is no need to cross it, as the towpath passes underneath. The little village of Drumbeg, with its old church and pub, is just a short way along the road, on the opposite side of the river. After passing under the road at Drum Bridge, turn left to cross a footbridge over the River Lagan, then turn right to follow the river upstream. You will be able to look across the river to Sir Thomas and Lady Dixon Park. The Lagan Canal Towpath follows the River Lagan for a while, but then detours left, and you pass through a concrete tunnel beneath the M1 motorway.

Next, a straight stretch of the old canal begins to waver, and you pass under a road bridge near

Ballyskeagh. The bridge is made of red sandstone, and features two high arches. One arch allows passage for the canal and the other takes the towpath. Continuing along the towpath, you pass a factory before reaching Lambeg Bridge. Just as you cross the road at Lambeg Bridge, you will be walking alongside a loop of the River Lagan, before the Lagan Canal Towpath follows the old canal cutting towards Lisburn. Although this final stretch remains tree-lined, you will become more aware of houses, schools and old mill buildings. The linen mill at Hilden dominates the waterside after you pass another road bridge.

The Lagan Canal at Ballyskeagh Bridge.

Don't be tempted to cross any of the footbridges on this final stretch, but stay on the southern bank of the river until you reach a wide road bridge. Turn right to cross this bridge, then cross the busy road beyond before walking straight up into Lisburn. The bus station and railway station are signposted in the town centre, although the Ulsterbus services to Belfast generally leave from Castle Street.

A quiet tree-lined stretch of the River Lagan.

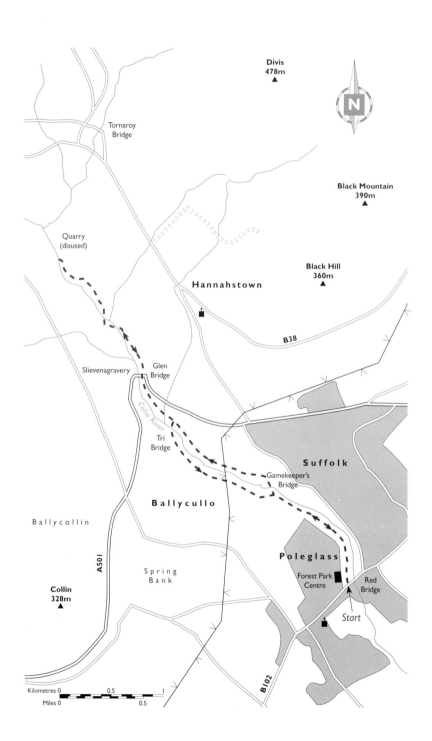

Divis
478m
▲

N

Black Mountain
390m
▲

Tornaroy
Bridge

Black Hill
360m
▲

Quarry
(disused)

Hannahstown

B38

Slievenagravery

Glen
Bridge

Colin River

Tri
Bridge

Suffolk

Gamekeeper's
Bridge

Ballycullo

Ballycollin

Poleglass

Spring
Bank

Forest Park
Centre

Red
Bridge

Collin
328m
▲

A501

Start

B102

Kilometres 0   0.5   1
Miles 0   0.5

COLIN GLEN

Older residents in West Belfast know this as McCance's Glen, after a family who bleached linen nearby in the 1770s. In 1881, the McCances drew water from the mountain stream to power a mill on Suffolk Road. In those days, the glen featured an ancient woodland where the trees slowly, but constantly regenerated themselves.

Stouppe Finlay McCance was an outdoors man, and from 1890 until 1926 he managed the glen for fishing and shooting, employing a gamekeeper and other men for pheasant shoots. In the 1940s, the lower glen was clear-felled to provide wood for furniture-makers Gilpins on the Sandy Row. The National Trust, however, managed to acquire and save the upper glen. Later the lower glen was also used as a brickworks and a landfill site.

Colin Glen Forest Park owes its existence to a combination of natural forces and community involvement. Nature began work at restoring the tree cover, and as housing estates spread around both sides of the glen, the need for an amenity area grew. The tidying up of Colin Glen, and the creation of a network of splendid paths is all due to a cross-community project which has won awards and been recognised throughout Europe.

A recent addition has been the Colin Glen Forest Park Centre, which houses background information and a small restaurant. The centre is much used by local school groups, and is administered by the Colin Glen Trust. There is a car park, but if you use it, then be sure to let the staff know. Alternatively, there are frequent Ulsterbus City Stopper services passing the centre on Stewartstown Road.

Walk through the car park, passing the Forest Park Centre, to follow a broad and obvious path into the woods beyond. Although the glen is hemmed in by housing, you will often be unaware of the urban

INFORMATION

Distance: 3.5 or 5 km (2 or 3 miles), depending on whether you explore the upper glen.

Start and finish: Colin Glen Forest Park Centre on Stewartstown Road in West Belfast.

Terrain: Easy tarmac paths in the lower glen, for which ordinary shoes are fine, but rather rougher paths in the upper glen, where boots are recommended.

Public transport: Ulsterbus City Stoppers 530, 531, 532, 533, 537 and 538 pass Colin Glen Forest Park Centre.

Time: Allow about 1½ hours to explore the lower glen, or 2½ hours if you proceed into the upper glen.

Refreshments: Available at Colin Glen Forest Park Centre.

Opening hours: *Colin Glen Forest Park Centre:* Mon-Thu, 0900–1630, Fri 0900–1300. Admission free (01232 614115).

surroundings. When you emerge into a clearing, you will notice a red footbridge on the right, known as the Red Bridge, which leads onto Suffolk Road. Don't cross it, but continue following Colin River upstream.

The Red Bridge spanning Colin River.

You won't always be walking within sight of the river, but keep following clear paths through the trees and shrubs. As the woodland is relatively young, there is a lush ground cover. When you find a path heading off

Deep inside the wooded Colin Glen.

to the right (500 m after the Red Bridge), follow this across Colin River, crossing the Gamekeeper's Bridge, then walk further up the wooded glen. The next bridge you pass is the Weir Bridge. Don't cross it, but simply keep walking upstream.

The Tri Bridge is unusual; a modern structure where three paths actually meet on the bridge – hence its name. You will be drawn onto it, but don't cross over the river just yet. Keep right to continue further upstream. The next bridge is Glen Bridge – a large stone arch carrying a main road across the glen. A walkway runs under the bridge, allowing access to the upper glen.

If you are only out for a short stroll, then turn round at this point, but if you want a slightly longer walk and are wearing boots, then you can explore the upper glen. The National Trust owns this area, where the ancient woodland still survives and stands, in contrast to the recent developments in the lower glen.

To walk in the upper glen, climb uphill a short way from the Glen Bridge, then turn left to follow a narrow path upstream. There are steps in places, and after a while a wooden footbridge spans Colin River. Cross this bridge, and walk further upstream. You will notice what appear to be two tree trunks spanning the river – but in fact these are the remains of a former footbridge. Cross carefully between them, and expect to get wet feet.

A steep flight of steps leads uphill to the edge of the wood, where you turn left. After following a path along the inside edge of the wood, you will be drawn gradually down towards the river again, and eventually you can emerge at the head of the glen where an old quarry may in time be developed as another public amenity.

Walking through Colin Glen.

Turn around and walk back down through the glen, retracing your steps under the Glen Bridge and along the easier path to the curious Tri Bridge. Now you can cross the Tri Bridge and turn left to follow another path downstream. Although the path pulls away from Colin River, it is never too far from it. Avoid any left turns, which will either take you down to the Weir Bridge or the Gamekeeper's Bridge. Eventually you pass the Red Bridge and follow a path back to the Colin Glen Forest Park Centre.

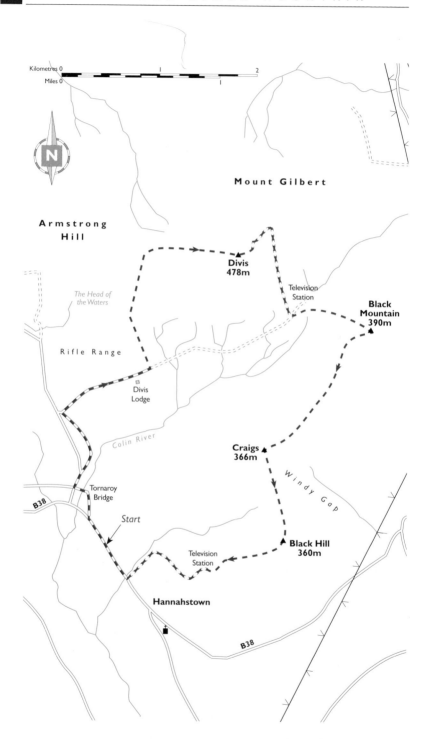

DIVIS AND BLACK MOUNTAIN

Divis and Black Mountain are the highest points on the Belfast Hills, and the city suburbs are gradually creeping up their flanks. There are tall transmitter masts on Black Hill, Black Mountain and Divis, and although these are unattractive to look at, they are nevertheless landmarks which prove useful when navigating from one point to another. In fact, you can use these masts

Davis and Black Mountain rise above Belfast.

to identify the summits even from the streets of Belfast. The access roads serving the masts offer easy walking at least partway across the moorland slopes, but there is also some boggy, pathless terrain to be covered.

This walk starts on the Upper Springfield Road above Hannahstown in West Belfast. Parking is limited. There are small spaces by the roadside, which are not particularly recommended. The only real car park is that which is attached to the Gaelic Football ground of Pairc Lámh Dhearg, although this would obviously not be available during matches. Alternatively, you could use the Ulsterbus service to reach the start.

To get the bulk of the road-walking over first, follow the busy Upper Springfield Road away from Pairc Lámh Dhearg, until you can walk along a wide, gravel track off to the right. This track passes a couple of

INFORMATION

Distance: 11 km (7 miles).

Start and finish: On the Upper Springfield Road at Hannahstown in West Belfast.

Terrain: Access roads serve transmission masts on Black Hill, Black Mountain and Divis, but there is a wet and boggy moorland to be crossed, and boots are recommended.

Public transport: Ulsterbus service 106 runs through Hannahstown.

Time: Allow 4 hours to complete the walk, allowing for a stretch of pathless moorland.

Refreshments: None actually on the route, but places to eat and drink can be found back towards the city.

Access Note: There is a firing range on the slopes of Divis, and if red flags are flying, then firing is taking place and you will not be able to climb the hill. Advance information about the likelihood of firing can be obtained from the Army Information Office at Lisburn, telephone (01846) 609674.

houses and crosses Tornaroy Bridge, then you turn right again to walk up a narrow tarmac road. The road climbs, and beyond the hedgerows there are views of the hills you will be traversing – along with their distinctive array of masts.

Follow the minor road uphill until you can turn right and cross a cattle grid to follow a narrow, unfenced road. There is a firing range off to the left, with a handful of small buildings associated with the range, and signs later warn you not to proceed if red flags are flying – although the range seems hardly ever to be in use. As the road climbs, you will pass the ruins of Divis Lodge, which was once a high-level farmstead.

Divis as seen from Legoniol Park.

A gravel track leads off to the left just after the lodge. Follow this track uphill, and as it climbs look out for a fork to the right; follow the track to its very end. You should notice a boundary ditch running across the moorland slopes in a straight line from Armstrongs Hill to Divis, and by turning right you can follow this feature up the grass and heather slopes of Divis.

An army installation crowns Divis, surrounded by coils of barbed wire. The 'No Entry' signs are superfluous as you probably wouldn't want to get in! Floodlights around the perimeter fence make the summit of Divis unmistakable even in distant views at night. Effectively, access is denied to the actual 478 m summit of Divis, which is the highest point in the Belfast Hills. If you wander around the perimeter fence, however, you can enjoy views across Belfast, Belfast Lough, the Antrim Mountains, Sperrin Mountains, Lough Neagh and the Mountains of Mourne. In clear weather, parts of Scotland can also be seen.

Getting onto Divis was simple enough, and leaving it is even easier. Just follow the tarmac access road downhill. There is a hairpin bend, overlooked by a security camera, then you walk straight down to a road junction near a tall mast on a gap between Divis and Black Mountain. Pass the mast by keeping to its right-hand side, crossing the boggy moorland before joining a firm, grassy track. Follow this track over the broad rise of Black Mountain and you can descend a short way to a trig pillar at 390 m. There is a fine view over Belfast's urban sprawl from the pillar.

Leave the summit by walking roughly south-west, and you will cross a stretch of boggy, undulating moorland before reaching a firmer footing on the minor hump of Craigs. Walk southwards from Craigs to cross a minor moorland gap, passing beneath an electricity transmission line on the way. A short walk uphill leads to another trig pillar at 360 m on the summit of Black Hill.

There are active and potentially dangerous quarries on the south-western slopes of Black Hill, but when you leave the summit you should aim more west-south-west to reach another tall transmitter mast on the slopes of the hill. There is a low fence to be crossed on the way, then you should keep to the right-hand side of the mast to join its access road. The access road leads straight down to the busy Upper Springfield Road at Hannahstown. If you are parked near Pairc Lámh Dhearg, you should turn right to retrieve your car; if you are catching a bus, make sure you stand at the right place at the right time, as services are rather limited.

Looking towards Divis from Black Hill.

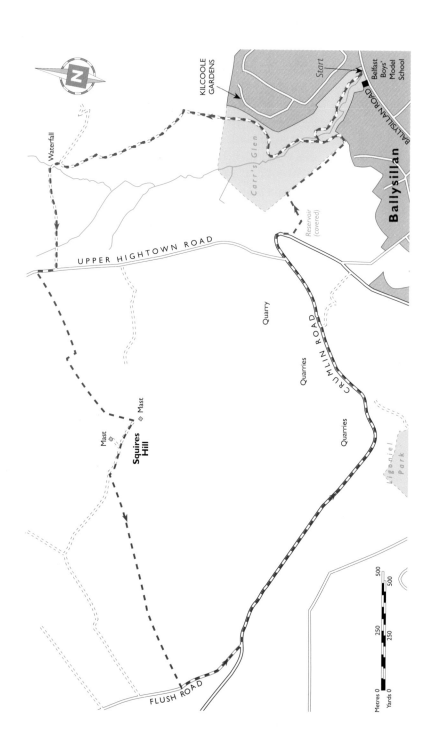

SQUIRES HILL

Squires Hill is in the middle of the Belfast Hills, and is readily distinguished because of its relative isolation and also because of the twin masts which have been planted on its summit. The whole southern side of Squires Hill has been quarried, and some quarries have subsequently been used for landfill sites. The suburbs of Belfast are gradually creeping up the southern slopes, and must surely stop spreading at some stage.

Start at Carr's Glen, which can be entered using a narrow tarmac access road running off Ballysillan Road just a short way downhill from the Belfast Boy's Model School. There is a small parking area at the end of this road, although you can also arrive using Citybus services and walk into the glen. As you enter the glen, Squires Hill rises directly ahead. A mapboard (unfortunately now barely legible) shows a series of short waymarked trails around the Cave Hill Country Park. If you can get a leaflet showing the course of these trails, it could prove quite useful.

There is a clear path running uphill from the car park, indicated by coloured waymark arrows carved on a large boulder. The path runs alongside a broad area of grass not far from a stream. Don't cross the stream when you reach a footbridge, but keep straight on, walking uphill along a gravel path. As this path climbs above the last of the houses at Kilcoole Gardens, you go through a gate and continue uphill along a fenced track.

When you reach a T-junction with another track, turn left and continue climbing gradually uphill. Follow the track left again across a small stream which features a little waterfall, and continue along the track to reach a car park beside Upper Hightown Road. Turn right to follow the road a short way uphill, then turn left to start climbing Squires Hill from a point opposite the entrance to a landfill site.

INFORMATION

Distance: 8 km (5 miles).

Start and finish: Carr's Glen, beside the Belfast Boy's Model School on Ballysillan Road in North Belfast.

Terrain: A mixture of firm tracks, hill paths which can be muddy, and some road walking. Boots recommended.

Public transport: Citybus services 35, 61 and 93 reach Carr's Glen.

Time: Allow about 3 hours for the ascent of and circuit around Squires Hill.

Refreshments: None on the course of the walk, but a couple of shops are available not far from the entrance to Carr's Glen.

Small waterfall above Carr's Glen.

The idea is to follow the line of a hedge and fence uphill, but avoiding a rather muddy area not long after leaving the road. Look out for a stile at a higher level and follow a fence towards the top of the hill. You can aim for the highest of the two transmitter masts on the summit, which is the one to the left, in a compound also containing the summit trig point at 374 m. There is a grand view from the summit across Belfast, and also to much more distant features such as the Mountains of Mourne, the Antrim Mountains, Sperrin Mountains and Lough Neagh. The Galloway Hills of Scotland may also be visible across Belfast Lough in clear weather.

Follow the access track downhill a short way from the two masts, but turn left when you reach an earth embankment which cuts across the hillside. Follow this mound gradually downhill, crossing a couple of stiles before crossing a wide field on the way down to Flush Road. Turn left along this minor road, then left again along Crumlin Road.

Line of trees running towards Squires Hill.

Follow this busy road downhill, walking on the pavement along its left side. The immediate scenery is not great, but there are fine views across the city spreading away far below. You need to follow Crumlin Road down until you reach a prominent sharp bend to the right. Just after turning this bend, there is a stile next to a gated access road on the left, where a small sign announces the Cave Hill Country Park.

Cross the stile and follow the access road towards a covered reservoir. Cross another stile on the left, then walk down to the lowest corner of a field. The ground can be very muddy where you pass from one field into the next. Turn right to walk down the side of this second field, until you cross a stile and reach the top side of the Belfast Boys' Model School. Turn left alongside the school fence and follow a path which crosses the stream in Carr's Glen. Turn right after crossing a footbridge and you will quickly land back at the car park near the entrance to the glen.

Squires Hill as seen from Ardoyne.

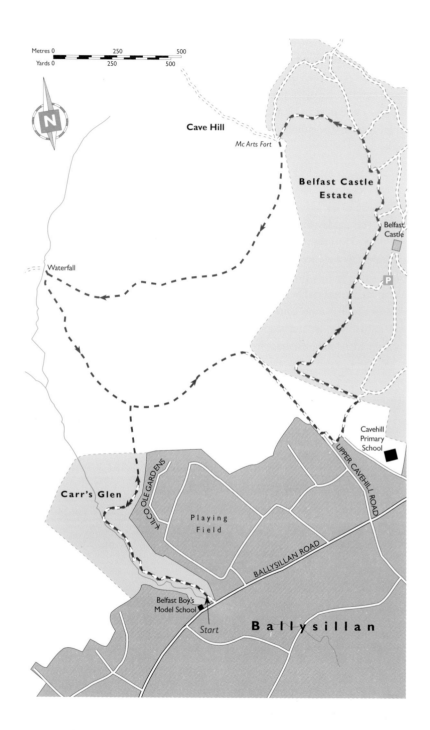

Metres 0 250 500
Yards 0 250 500

N

Cave Hill

Mc Arts Fort

Belfast Castle Estate

Belfast Castle

P

Waterfall

Cavehill Primary School

Carr's Glen

KICOOLE GARDENS

Playing Field

UPPER CAVEHILL ROAD

BALLYSILLAN ROAD

Belfast Boy's Model School

Start

B a l l y s i l l a n

CAVE HILL FROM CARR'S GLEN

Carr's Glen is a pleasant, but unremarkable little glen on the fringes of Belfast, and is part of the Cave Hill Country Park. Carr's Glen offers one approach to Cave Hill – other approaches being commonly made from Belfast Castle or Belfast Zoo. The route is structured to run within sight of Belfast Castle, so that you can detour to visit the place if you wish. Three upper rooms in the castle have been set aside as the Cave Hill Heritage Centre, giving plenty of background information about the area.

Cave Hill Country Park has been created from a number of estates which have come into public ownership. Carr's Glen is one such area, and others include the Belfast Castle Estate, the Wallace Estate, Hazelwood and Bellevue. The Country Park is managed by Belfast Parks Department. There are frequent Citybus services to Carr's Glen, and you will find the entrance to the glen just next to the Belfast Boys' Model School. A short way along the access road is a car park, if you choose to arrive by car. The lower part of the glen features a small stream, young trees and shrubs, and an open area of grass.

Follow an obvious path away from the car park, staying fairly close to the stream at first. Don't follow the path across the stream when it suddenly turns left to cross a footbridge. Instead, walk straight onwards and upwards along a clear gravel path. Follow this path uphill, and keep bearing to the right to climb more steeply uphill above the last of the houses at Kilcoole Gardens on the hillside.

A fenced track runs straight uphill and reaches a T-junction with another track. Turn right and walk gradually downhill. Make sure you turn left at the next junction of tracks to enter an area of pleasant mixed woodland. By staying on the clearest track, you will be drawn through the woods and out onto Upper Cavehill Road. You don't need to follow the actual road, as there is a path running downhill just alongside.

INFORMATION

Distance: 8 km (5 miles).

Start and finish: Carr's Glen, beside the Belfast Boy's Model School on Ballysillan Road in North Belfast.

Terrain: Hillside and woodlands, mostly featuring firm and clear paths, but boots are recommended.

Public transport: Citybus services 35, 61 and 93 reach Carr's Glen.

Time: Allow 2½ to 3 hours, or longer if you detour to visit Belfast Castle.

Refreshments: A few shops near the start on Ballysillan Road, otherwise there is a restaurant at Belfast Castle just off route.

Opening hours: *Cave Hill Heritage Centre, Belfast Castle:* daily, 0900–1800. Admission free (01232 776925).

Turn left a short way down this path to re-enter the mixed woodlands. You are now in the grounds of the Belfast Castle Estate, and by keeping left you will be

able to follow a clear and firm path uphill. This path later bends to the right, and any other paths leading off to the right would take you down to Belfast Castle if you wished to visit the place. If not, then keep left at any junctions, and you will have a fleeting glimpse of the castle anyway.

Walk along the clearest woodland path, remembering to keep turning left and climbing gradually up through the woods. Eventually, the trees thin out on the slopes beneath the frowning cliffs of Cave Hill. Leave the gravel path and follow another trodden path off to the left, which climbs more steeply uphill for

McArt's Fort on Cave Hill guarded by cliffs.

a short while. You will notice it leads towards a prominent cave – one of a series cut into the flanks of Cave Hill. It is thought that these were early iron mines.

Looking across the lower slopes of Cave Hill.

Don't walk all the way up to the cave mouth, unless you want to explore it, but turn left and follow another

path uphill and across the steep hillside. Avoid a badly eroded scar, which can prove awkward to cross, and follow a path at a higher level towards a prominent notch at the top of the cliff line. This notch is actually an ancient ditch associated with a promontory fort on top of the cliff, where you are aiming to stand.

This is McArt's Fort, where you can enjoy an amazing panorama over the city of Belfast, but take care of the cliffs which fall precipitously on most sides. This point has also been called Ben Madigan, after an Ulster king of the 9th

Part of the defensive ditch at McArt's Fort.

century, and Napoleon's Nose, after its resemblance in profile to the nose of the famous general and emperor!

There is a clear gravel path running along the southern cliff tops, and this is the path which returns you to Carr's Glen. Follow the path along the top of the slope, near the moorland edge, until it descends more steeply to pass areas of thorny scrub. Keep always to the clearest path until you reach a track crossing a stream, where you should notice a small waterfall off to the right.

Turn sharply left, without crossing the stream, to follow another clear gravel track downhill. After an initial steep descent, the track gradient eases, and you will notice another track leading downhill to the right. This track was used at the start of the day's walk, and you simply let it lead you back down into Carr's Glen to end the walk. This walk can of course be combined with the following walk over Cave Hill to create a longer circular walk.

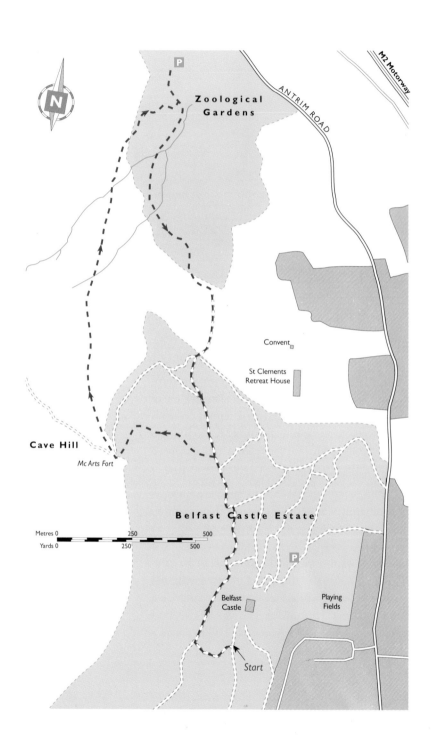

N

M2 Motorway

P

**Zoological
Gardens**

ANTRIM ROAD

Convent

St Clements
Retreat House

Cave Hill

Mc Arts Fort

Belfast Castle Estate

Metres 0   250   500

Yards 0   250   500

P

Belfast
Castle

Playing
Fields

Start

CAVE HILL FROM BELFAST CASTLE

Cave Hill, which has stood through the ages, frowns on Belfast Castle, a late 19th century upstart of a building. Constructed by the Donegall family in the 1870s, the castle and its estate

Belfast Castle and Cave Hill.

were handed over to Belfast Corporation in 1934. It now forms the main visitor centre for the Cave Hill Country Park.

Three upper rooms in Belfast Castle have been set aside as the Cave Hill Heritage Centre. This interesting permanent exhibition offers plenty of background about Cave Hill, including its geology, archaeology, natural history and Victorian curiosity value. The centre includes a closed circuit television camera mounted on top of the castle, which allows you to pan around the area and zoom in on selected features. Leaflets are available detailing a series of short waymarked trails through the country park.

Belfast Castle and Cave Hill Country Park are signposted from the Antrim Road, which is as near as you can get using regular Citybus services. If you arrive by bus, you will have to walk along the suburban road of Inisfayle Park to reach the access road for Belfast Castle. If you arrive by car, drive into the estate via Inisfayle Park and stop at a small car park before you reach a barrier gate near the castle.

INFORMATION

Distance: 6 km (4 miles).

Start and finish: Belfast Castle, which is reached as signposted from the Antrim Road via Inisfayle Park.

Terrain: Mostly clear paths, but some are steep, and may be muddy in wet weather, so boots are recommended.

Public transport: Citybus services 2 to 6, 8 to 10 and 45 run along Antrim Road passing Inisfayle Park, which leads to Belfast Castle.

Time: Allow 2½ hours, or much longer if you intend to visit Belfast Castle or Belfast Zoo.

Refreshments: There are restaurants at Belfast Castle, and Belfast Zoo, although to use the one at the zoo you will need to pay an admission charge first.

Opening hours: *Cave Hill Heritage Centre, Belfast Castle:* daily, 0900–1800. Admission free (01232 776925). *Belfast Zoo:* Apr-Sep, daily, 1000–1700. Oct-Mar, daily, 1000–1530. Admission charge (01232 776277).

You can visit the castle if you like, or launch yourself straight into the climb up Cave Hill. The path running up to Cave Hill starts immediately from the car park, climbing up to a T-junction of gravel paths where you turn right. The path allows a view of Belfast Castle before running through mature mixed woodlands. There are other paths in the woods, but all you need to do is to keep left along the most obvious paths as you climb gradually up through the woods.

Belfast Castle and its ornamental gardens.

When the path leaves the woods, look out for another trodden path climbing more steeply to the left. It runs towards a cave in the foot of the rugged cliffs of Cave Hill. Walk up to the cave mouth if you wish to explore it, or turn left along another path beforehand. You need to climb fairly steeply uphill to a notch on the skyline, but avoiding a patch of badly eroded hillside. The notch turns out to be part of the defensive works associated with the ancient promontory fort of McArt's Fort on Cave Hill. Beware of cliffs falling sheer from McArt's Fort, and enjoy an amazing urban panorama across Belfast, its docks and its sprawling suburbs. It was on Cave Hill that Wolfe Tone and the United Irishmen took their solemn oath to free Ireland in the run-up to the Rebellion of 1798.

After sampling the view from McArt's Fort, leave by following the path along the northern cliff line. This path is quite clear on the ground, but can be muddy in places after rain. On the descent, you will cross a couple of small streams before entering the wooded nature reserve of Hazelwood. The path steepens and narrows as it goes down the wooded slope. After following a cobbly path and flights of steps downhill, you turn left along the perimeter fence of Belfast Zoo until you reach the entrance gate.

Sheer cliffs falling from McArt's Fort

If you want to visit the zoo, this is your chance. If you don't, walk back along the side of the fence and go up the first flight of steps, before turning left. There is a path which is sometimes just above, and sometimes just beside the perimeter fence. Follow this wooded path gradually uphill until it leaves the upper part of the zoo and proceeds across an open hillside. Now that you have a clear view of your surroundings, you will recognise the dramatic cliffs of Cave Hill again.

The path runs down into the mixed woodlands you passed through at the beginning of the walk, and all you need to do is follow the clearest paths through the woods, turning right until you have a view of Belfast Castle. After that, a left turn leads straight back down to the car park near Belfast Castle.

This walk can be combined with the previous ascent of Cave Hill from Carr's Glen to create a longer circular walk. The Ulster Way crosses Cave Hill, and its course was used on the descent from McArt's Fort to Belfast Zoo.

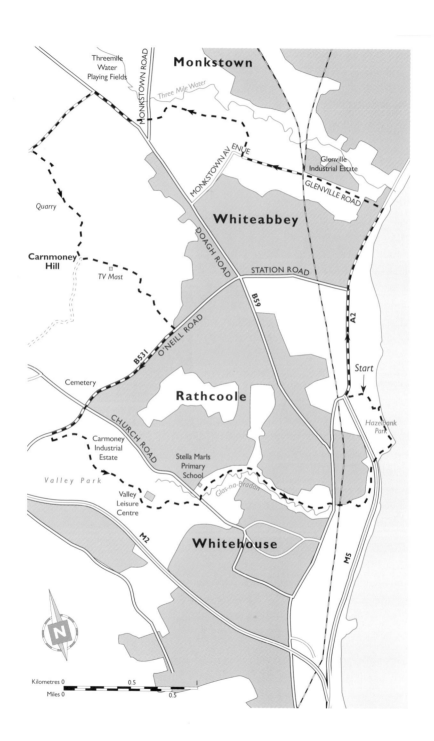

CARNMONEY HILL

This route includes a couple of parks, a hillwalk, a riverside path, a coastal walk and a stretch of the Ulster Way; all within the suburbs of Newtownabbey. There are regular Ulsterbus services to and from Belfast, as well as a railway service to Whiteabbey, or you can park at the start of the walk just inside Hazelbank Park.

The walk starts and finishes near Belfast Lough.

If you come by car, walk back towards the roundabout on the main road at the park entrance. An Ulster Way signpost points to the right, so that you don't have to walk alongside the busy Shore Road until later. If you arrive by Ulsterbus, start walking near the East Antrim Institute college building, following the Shore Road towards Whiteabbey. If you arrive by train at Whiteabbey Station, follow Station Road onto Shore Road and turn left to begin the walk.

Just as you draw close to a war memorial on a coastal green, look out for Glenville Road running inland to the left. Take this road underneath a railway arch and past an industrial estate. Follow the road almost to a junction with Monkstown Avenue, but turn right before this point to follow a track towards a row of houses. Don't walk to the houses, but continue along a narrow path which later runs around the perimeter fence of a bus depot.

INFORMATION

Distance: 13 km (8 miles).

Start and finish: Hazelbank Park, at the northern end of the M5 motorway near Whiteabbey.

Terrain: Mostly roads, tracks and firm paths, but also some muddy patches where boots would be useful.

Public transport: Citybus City Express services 1A and 1B, and Ulsterbus services 163 and 166 pass Hazelbank Park. Northern Ireland Railways also serve Whiteabbey on the line between Belfast and Larne.

Time: Allow 4–5 hours for the circuit. Bus services can be used to shorten the walk.

Refreshments: Surprisingly, for such a suburban walk, there is very little. A few shops can be found along the busy Shore Road near the start.

Carnmoney Hill seen across Belfast Lough.

The path becomes a broad track, passing the Monkstown Industrial Estate to run into Monkstown Road. Cross straight over the road and follow a leafy track straight up onto Doagh Road. Turn right, but only as far as the next crossroads, then turn left up Ballyduff Road. One steep and narrow part of this road is one-way only before the road carries two-way traffic at a higher level.

There are two access roads together on the left. Go along the first one, which is a concrete lane, and avoid the second, which serves a landfill site. Just before you reach a house, turn right at a gateway and follow another concrete lane uphill. There is another gate along this lane, with a stile alongside, before you let the lane lead you to a transmitter mast on top of Carnmoney Hill at 207 m.

Walk off the end of the concrete lane to cross a stile straight ahead. There is a rough and brambly slope to go down before you cross another stile. Keep going downhill and look ahead to spot a vague path on the slopes of scrubby woodland and grassy areas. By keeping to the left of a roadside filling station you should locate a dilapidated stile which needs to be crossed before you can finally walk down onto O'Neill Road.

Turn right to follow O'Neill Road to a roundabout beside Carnmoney Cemetery. Go straight through the roundabout and stay on O'Neill Road until you can turn left to enter Valley Park, where a small car park is located. Turn left again to follow a clear tarmac path around a broad area of grass, and keep left at a triangular junction of paths.

Switch to a concrete path going left, then keep right to walk along an embankment overlooking a small wildfowl pond. Keep to the right of a large building ahead – the Valley Leisure Centre – and follow its access road away to

Gideon's Green, named after a diarist.

Church Road. Cross over Church Road near a filling station and turn left, then almost immediately turn right to pass a sign for the Ulster Way and Glas na Bradan – the stream of the silvery trout.

Glas na Bradan is one of many areas in the city suburbs which have been tidied up and improved through cross-community employment schemes. In this area, between Whitehouse and Rathcoole, a continuous path has been created along the wooded banks of the stream. Simply follow the path downstream to Shore Road, but don't cross over the stream at any point.

Cross Shore Road with care; there is a bend where visibility is limited. Go under a railway arch and walk beside a tidal lagoon. A tarmac path leads off to the right, and if you bear right again you can follow a concrete path across Gideon's Green. You will pass a memorial boulder which explains how the green got its name from a diarist who recorded the landing of Williamite troops nearby in 1689.

The path runs beneath the busy M5 motorway, and continues around Macedon Point to reach Hazelbank Park. To return to the car park and the entrance to Hazelbank Park, look out for an Ulster Way signpost just before a stone tower rising from the shore, then follow the most obvious path inland to end back at the car park. Continue onto the main road if you need to catch a bus, or along Shore Road until you turn onto Station Road if you are catching a train.

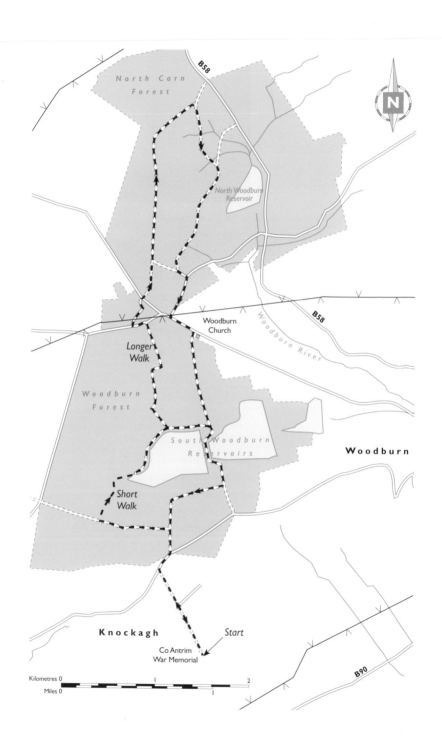

North Carn Forest

B58

North Woodburn Reservoir

B58

Woodburn River

Woodburn Church

Longer Walk

Woodburn Forest

South Woodburn Reservoirs

Woodburn

Short Walk

Knockagh

Co Antrim War Memorial

Start

Kilometres 0   1   2

Miles 0   1

B90

N

KNOCKAGH AND WOODBURN FOREST

The County Antrim War Memorial is a landmark all around Belfast Lough, and far beyond, standing as it does on top of the steep escarpment at Knockagh between Newtownabbey and Carrickfergus. The Ulster Way runs close to it on its way from Newtownabbey to Ballynure, charting a course through Woodburn Forest and North Carn Forest.

Knockagh is worth visiting for the splendid views it offers across Belfast Lough, and you can follow the nearby Ulster Way into Woodburn Forest on this walk. A short and easy circuit is offered, and if you want to extend it, then you can proceed further along

The County Antrim War Memorial at Knockagh.

INFORMATION

Distance: 7 or 14 km (4.5 or 9 miles) depending on whether you include North Carn Forest.

Start and finish: At the County Antrim War Memorial at Knockagh, high above Greenisland.

Terrain: Mostly hard forest tracks or minor roads, but some muddy paths, so boots are recommended.

Public transport: There are no buses serving this walk, but Ulsterbus service 165 from Carrickfergus runs to Woodburn, where roads can be followed uphill to join the route at either Knockagh or Woodburn Church.

Time: Allow 2 hours for the shorter walk, or 4 hours for the longer walk.

Refreshments: Nothing at all on the route. Head for Carrickfergus after the walk to find a full range of facilities.

Opening hours: *The War Memorial, Woodburn Forest and North Carn Forest are always open. Admission free.*

the Ulster Way to visit North Carn Forest. Knockagh is reached by following a minor road between Woodburn and Monkstown, and there is a small car park at the end of the access road. The memorial was raised after the First World War, and the views from it stretch well beyond Belfast Lough to the Mountains of Mourne and the hills of Galloway in Scotland.

Walk back down the road from the memorial, noting the beech hedges which have been planted alongside the road. In 1 km, turn right along a minor road and in a further 200 m, left at an Ulster Way marker to follow a track into Woodburn Forest. Turn left in 200 m along another track and cross a small stream. You might notice a narrow path leading off to the right, but you don't actually follow it. Instead, follow the forest track over a rise, then take another narrow path off to the right. This path runs through the forest and can be muddy underfoot, but in 500 m it leads straight to the head of South Woodburn Reservoir.

Turn right after crossing a concrete bridge over an inflowing stream and follow a track alongside South Woodburn Reservoir for 900 m. There are two tracks on the left leading away from the reservoir shore. Turn left along the second one, if you want to complete the longer walk, or continue straight towards the dam of the reservoir if you only want a short walk.

The longer walk takes in the neighbouring North Carn Forest. The track leading away from the reservoir joins another forest track in 200 m, where you turn right, then in 400 m right again at the following junction. After that, almost immediately on the left, is a path which leads in 400 m to a minor road called Lisglass Road.

Turn left to follow the road a few paces, then turn right to enter another block of forest using a track. The track soon dwindles to a path before you reach another minor road. Turn left on this road too, then right to follow the next forest track. This track runs practically straight northwards through North Carn Forest. In 1.6 km, you pass a waymark post where the Ulster Way turns left, away from the forest track. Stay

Previous page;
A woodland corner in
autumn.

on the track, however, for a further 500 m, and turn sharply right onto another track to complete this walk. Most of this end of North Carn Forest has been clear felled and replanted. The track you follow keeps right at one junction in 600 m, then left at the next in 1.1km to lead you out of the forest.

Turn right along the Councillors Road, then in 400 m left along the next road to pass a sign reading 'Woodburn Church'. You will later see the Presbyterian Church on the right-hand side of the road, and at that point you turn right to follow a clear track running back into Woodburn Forest. Follow this track straight downhill for 1km to land between the two South Woodburn Reservoirs.

Whether you are completing the short or the long walk, you follow the track which runs between the two reservoirs, and even walk a short way along the side of the lower reservoir. Turn right to follow a forest track uphill, away from the lower reservoir. Turn right again along this track, then in 500 m turn left and walk uphill to return to the minor road you were using earlier in the day. Turn right along the road to walk away from the forest, then left to follow the road back up to the war memorial at Knockagh for one last look at the view.

The route alongside South Woodburn Reservoir.

This forested stretch of the Ulster Way is flanked by road walking in both directions. You could follow the Ulster Way back towards Belfast by way of Newtownabbey, or continue onwards to pass through the village of Ballynure on the way to the Antrim Mountains. If you are looking for nearby refreshments after completing the walk, then a visit to Carrickfergus is recommended. Carrickfergus Castle and the Knight Ride Centre offer plenty of background history and heritage, while portions of the ancient town walls can be studied as you wander around the town centre.

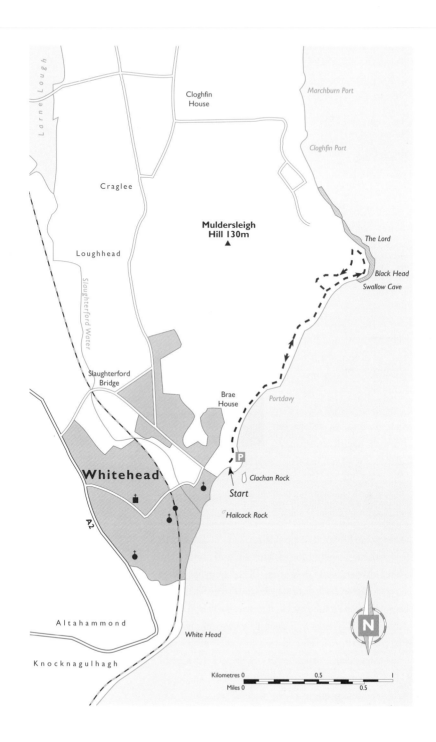

Lorne Lough

Cloghfin
House

Marchburn Port

Cloghfin Port

C r a g l e e

L o u g h h e a d

Slaughterford Water

**Muldersleigh
Hill 130m**
▲

The Lord

Black Head
Swallow Cave

Slaughterford
Bridge

Brae
House

Portdavy

P

Whitehead

Clachan Rock

Start

Hailcock Rock

A2

A l t a h a m m o n d

White Head

K n o c k n a g u l h a g h

Kilometres 0		0.5		1
Miles 0			0.5	

N

WHITEHEAD AND BLACK HEAD

Whitehead is a small seaside town at the mouth of Belfast Lough, while nearby Black Head overlooks both Belfast Lough and the North Channel. If you arrive at the appropriate time, then you could inspect steam engines at the headquarters of the Railway Preservation Society of Ireland. The Portrush Flyer is

Turning around the point of Black Head.

sometimes available for steam-hauled excursions around the countryside. There are both bus and rail services to Whitehead, as well as parking for cars – all of which are close to the start of the walk to Black Head.

The Black Head Path is a remarkable construction, which has been cut into, or built onto the rugged cliffs at the mouth of Belfast Lough. This rocky headland would be almost impossible to cover on foot without the path, and in recent years the walkway was getting quite weather-beaten and dilapidated. However, the lower path was largely reconstructed in 1993 and offers a safe, but spectacular walk. Flights of steps lead up to the lighthouse on top of the headland, then more steps lead back down onto the lower path. The whole walk is easily accomplished from Whitehead.

Start on the Promenade at any point in Whitehead, turning left to walk towards the mouth of Belfast Lough. There is a good path along the Promenade, and there is also a car park at the end of the

Promenade if you prefer to start there. There is an impressive list of small-print bye-laws on a noticeboard if you have the time or inclination to study them.

The path running towards Black Head is entirely concrete, and is perfectly clear to follow, so route directions are hardly necessary. There are benches where you can rest and take things easy, as well as occasional shelters if you need protection from the weather. The beach below the path is mainly pebbly and features a number of large boulders, while the slopes rising inland are covered in a mixture of scrub and shrubs. Later, you pass in front of a couple of houses – beyond which Black Head begins to dominate the scene almost exclusively.

The path remains obvious and easy, no matter how rugged Black Head may seem. The path is a great feat of engineering considering the nature of the terrain. It has been cut into solid rock, which sometimes overhangs you and provides shelter from the rain.

Black Head falls sheer into Belfast Lough.

Footbridges span awesome gulfs and chasms where the surging sea sucks and slurps at the seaweed-covered rocks. Handrails and safety barriers give a sense of security. Flights of steps run up and down to take advantage of the easiest line. This walk would be inadvisable in gale-force winds, when waves might sometimes wash over the path.

After turning completely around the headland, flights of steps lead uphill, zig-zagging across the rugged slope. Taken steadily the steps are easy enough, but if you try to rush them, you will reach the top puffing and blowing. There is a lighthouse on Black Head, and the path passes in front of it, hemmed in between tall stone walls. Presumably, if you walk here at night a torch is hardly going to be necessary! Views from Black Head stretch along the length of Belfast Lough, and may also take in the Galloway Hills of Scotland, and maybe even the Isle of Man in clear weather.

Follow the path around the top of Black Head. At one point you will be walking parallel to the access road which serves the lighthouse. Soon afterwards, the path begins to descend through patches of scrub on steep slopes, and there are more flights of steps. Simply follow the path as it zig-zags downhill, and you will rejoin the lower path which you were following earlier. Turn right to walk by the two houses also passed earlier, and retrace your steps to Whitehead. There are plenty of places to eat and drink in town.

Black Head seen from across Belfast Lough.

This short coastal walk stands very much in isolation, but is one of the best little walks alongside Belfast Lough. For dedicated coastal walkers, it is the opposite side of Belfast Lough which should be visited, where the North Down Coastal Walk can be enjoyed – either in its entirety, or in short sections.

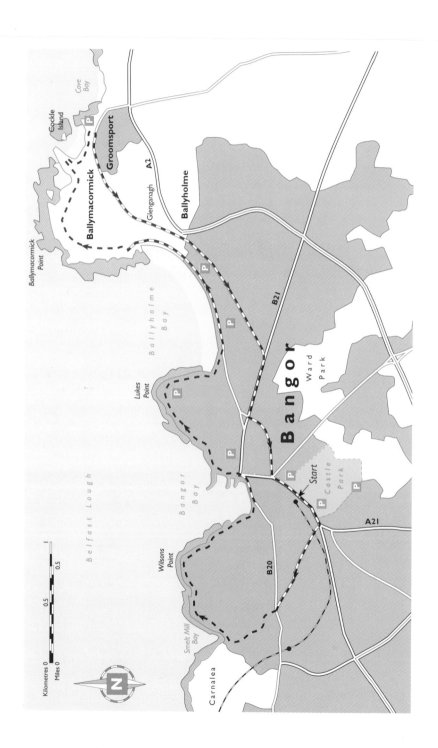

BANGOR AND GROOMSPORT

Bangor's history spans centuries, yet it retains the air of a genteel Victorian seaside resort. The entire harbour area has been reconstructed and now features a modern marina, with new stonework, brickwork, metalwork and planted areas of shrubs and flowers. Moving inland and uphill from the harbour are the main shopping streets and residential

INFORMATION

Distance: 15 km (9 miles), although the route is easily shortened.

Start and finish: At Castle Park – an open area just above the town centre in Bangor, near the bus and railway stations.

Terrain: Roads are used in the town of Bangor, while the coastal path varies from smooth tarmac to sandy beaches.

Public transport: Northern Ireland Railways operate between Belfast and Bangor. Ulsterbus services 1 and 2 link Belfast and Bangor, while Ulsterbus service 3 links Bangor and Groomsport.

Time: Allow around 5 or 6 hours to complete the walk, although there are obvious ways to shorten the distance.

Refreshments: Many places to eat and drink in Bangor, and a few places in Groomsport.

Opening hours: *North Down Heritage Centre, Castle Park Avenue, Bangor:* Jul-Aug, Mon-Sat, 1030–1730, Sun 1400–1730. Sep-Jun, Mon-Sat, 1030–1630, Sun 1400–1630, and Bank Holidays. Admission free (01247 271200).

Walking around the marina at Bangor.

areas. In the middle of it all is Castle Park, where the bus station and railway station are complemented by a car park.

This walk starts and finishes at Castle Park, in an attempt to turn a linear walk along part of the North Down Coastal Path into a circular walk. There is fairly easy access to the coastal path from Castle Park, and

by the time you reach Groomsport you have the option of catching a bus back to Bangor if you object to walking back along the road.

Whether you arrive by bus, train or car, you start walking from Castle Park, following Abbey Street and Brunswick Road towards the edge of town. When you reach a roundabout, look for the narrow Glen Road, which leads down to Strickland's Glen. There are a number of paths down through the wooded glen, and you can follow whichever you like until you reach the North Down Coastal Path. Maybe you will choose to follow the paths which run closest to Bryans Burn.

Turn right to follow the coastal path, which is a broad tarmac path only a step away from a jagged, rocky shore. The path runs below an old stone tower on a rocky, wooded slope, then turns around Wilson's Point to reach Pickie – where a number of children's entertainments are available. These include a narrow gauge railway and a boating lake with swan pedal-boats. Continue walking all the way around the harbour, which has been reconstructed into a well-stocked marina.

There are many opportunities to break for food and drink as you walk around the marina, and you can choose from a range of shops, pubs, cafes and restaurants. It is also possible to walk inland and uphill along the Main Street to return to Castle Park if you are content simply with a short stroll.

The frontages of the buildings around the marina look smart and colourful, but later you should look out for the much older Tower House which serves as the Tourist Information Centre. The Tower House was originally a customs house and was built in 1637. Continue along the road above the shore, or walk along a generous broad strip of grass where this is available. Eventually you turn the end of Lukes Point to reach the broad sweep of Ballyholme Bay.

Follow the promenade path around Ballyholme Bay until you reach a small children's play area at the end.

Opposite:
At the Mouth of
Strickland's Glen.

Beyond this point, you need to continue the walk while the tide is out – or at least while it isn't fully in – as you have to walk along a length of sandy beach. A wall rises from the beach, so you can't walk on dry land, but when you reach the far end of the wall you can come ashore onto a rough path leading to Ballymacormick Point.

The walk around Ballymacormick Point is on National Trust property, and features areas of rough grassland and patches of thorny scrub, which are being managed by selective grazing. Stay on the clearest path, which may be muddy or stony in places. When you finally reach the bay at Groomsport, turn right along a track, then left to reach the harbour. Groomsport was where 10,000 Williamite troops landed with Schomberg in 1689 before a series of famous battles fought throughout Ireland.

You could catch a bus back to Bangor, or walk back by road and complete the full distance. If you choose to return by road, then leave Groomsport via the minor Bangor Road. When you reach a roundabout on the edge of Ballyholme, keep away from the busy dual-carriageway East Circular Road and instead follow Groomsport Road back towards town. Later, turn right along Donaghadee Road, then left along Hamilton Road to return towards Castle Park and the bus and rail stations.

Opposite:
The Tower House and
Tourist Information
Centre.

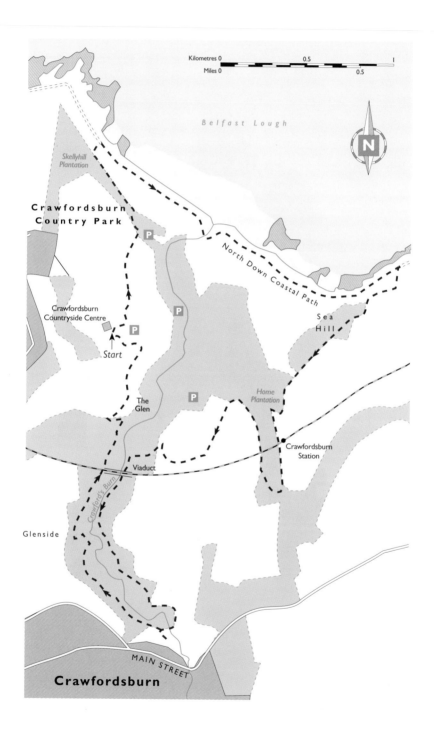

CRAWFORDSBURN COUNTRY PARK

Crawfordsburn Country Park is one of the busiest countryside sites in Northern Ireland. Situated on the shore of Belfast Lough between Holywood and Bangor, the area features a rocky coastline with sandy beaches, flowery meadows sprinkled with woodland, and a deep glen featuring a fine waterfall at its head. To help with countryside interpretation, there is an interesting and well-equipped visitor centre.

While it is possible to drive to Crawfordsburn Country Park and leave your car in one of many parking bays, it is also possible to arrive by Ulsterbus or rail services, in which case you could alter your starting point to suit. The suggested walk passes the railway station and runs very close to Crawfordsburn village, where Ulsterbus services pass. If starting from the village, do have a look at the Old Inn, which claims to be the oldest inn in Ireland, dating from 1614.

There are three waymarked trails which can be followed through the country park – the Coastal Walk, Meadow Walk and Glen Walk. A combination of parts of all three trails makes a fine, short, varied walk around the area, and the long distance Ulster Way also passes through the country park. If you want any background information, or food and drink, then it is best to start at the Crawfordsburn Countryside Centre.

Just outside the centre is a large sign listing the three waymarked trails, for which separate leaflets are available, and if you turn left along a path you will be able to

INFORMATION

Distance: 5 km (3 miles) combining a series of short waymarked trails.

Start and finish: Crawfordsburn Countryside Centre, although you can alter the starting point if arriving by bus or train.

Terrain: Mostly on firm, clear, dry gravel paths through meadows, along the coast and through woodlands, but wear boots in wet weather.

Public transport: Northern Ireland Railways serve Crawfordsburn from Belfast or Bangor. Ulsterbus services 1 and 2 reach Crawfordsburn, but check the timetables as not every bus passes through the village.

Time: Allow 1½ to 2 hours at least to explore this varied country park.

Refreshments: The Old Inn, Crawfordsburn. The Countryside Centre has a restaurant, but it is not always open.

Opening hours: *Crawfordsburn Country Park:* open daily until dusk. Admission free. *Crawfordsburn Countryside Centre:* Jun-Sep, daily, 0900–1830. Oct-May, daily, 0900–1700. Admission free (01247 853621).

Waymarked trails signposted at Crawfordsburn

The Coastal Walk at Crawfordsburn Country Park.

follow the blue waymark arrows for the Coastal Walk. This route follows a path gently downhill across a broad meadow, then turns left and climbs gently into a wooded area. A short stretch of path zig-zags down towards a rocky point, where you turn right to follow the rocky shoreline.

The Coastal Walk actually turns left and heads for Helen's Bay, but by turning right you can walk alongside Crawfordsburn Beach to cross a footbridge, then join the Meadow Walk, which is waymarked with green arrows. Turn left after crossing the footbridge and follow the path to the next low, rocky, wooded point. At this point, the Meadow Walk turns sharply right and climbs inland from Swineley Bay.

The Meadow Walk climbs up through a couple of grassy meadows which are separated by trees. The path reaches a narrow tarmac road, where you turn left and walk uphill. Follow the road under the railway line at Crawfordsburn Station, and later turn right and leave the road to cross a stone bridge over a stream. The track you follow then crosses the railway line.

Immediately after crossing the railway, turn left into a wildflower meadow and walk down the edge of it. The meadow was created by scraping off the topsoil before seeding, and the area is cut each year after natural seeding. Among the flowers you may see here in summer are buttercups, speedwell, ox-eye daisy and ragged robin. Turn left again after leaving the wildflower meadow and walk through an area of grassy patches separated by lines of trees. If you find yourself wondering about the curious layout of this area, then note that it was once a campsite. A narrow tarmac track leaves the former campsite and runs downhill.

There are several paths ahead, but you should keep left and follow a path upstream alongside Crawford's Burn. This is part of the Glen Walk, which is waymarked with red arrows. The Glen Walk passes beneath the tall stone arch of a railway viaduct. There are a couple of footbridges, but don't cross them; although you will have to cross one last footbridge and climb a few steps to view a fine waterfall at the head of the glen. The Old Inn at Crawfordsburn is just above this waterfall.

After admiring the waterfall, retrace your steps slightly and keep left to proceed downstream. Notice how the steep slopes of the glen have had to be stabilised to prevent landslips completely closing the path. Follow the path downstream, looking out for the red waymark arrows. These arrows will lead you across two narrow access roads on the way back towards the Crawfordsburn Countryside Centre and car parks.

Waterfall at the head of the Glen Walk.

The Ulster Way runs through Crawfordsburn Country Park and could be followed in either direction to offer a longer walk. It runs concurrent with the North Down Coastal Path from Crawfordsburn to Holywood, while you could also follow it inland to reach Helen's Tower, Newtownards and Scrabo Hill on the way to Strangford Lough.

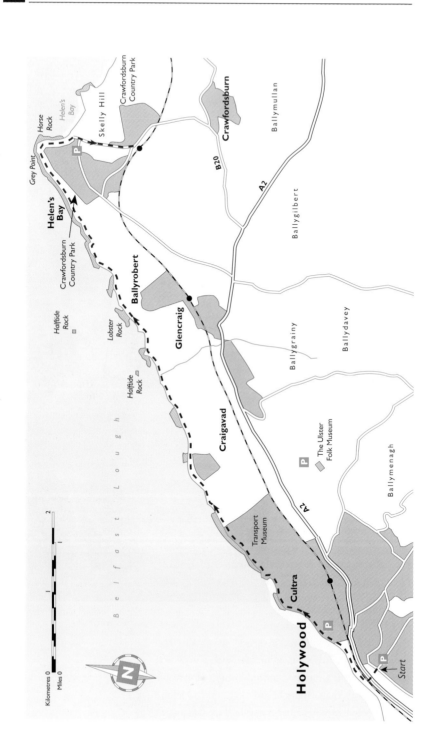

Kilometres 0 | 1 | 2
Miles 0 | 1

Belfast Lough

Grey Point
Horse Rock
Helen's Bay
Helen's Bay
Crawfordsburn Country Park
Skelly Hill
Crawfordsburn Country Park
Crawfordsburn

Halftide Rock
Lobster Rock
Crawfordsburn Country Park
Ballyrobert
Glencraig
Halftide Rock

Ballymullan
B20
A2
Ballygilbert
Ballygrainy
Ballydavey

Craigavad
The Ulster Folk Museum
Ballymenagh

Transport Museum
A2
Cultra
Holywood
Start

HOLYWOOD TO HELEN'S BAY

You can park in Holywood, or use either rail or Ulsterbus services to reach the town from Belfast or Bangor. Ideally, you should start walking from the centre of Holywood, if only to admire the world's tallest permanent maypole at a crossroads. It rises like a ship's mast for 20 m and replaces earlier maypoles dating back to the 17th century. Follow Shore Road down to a busy dual-

The promenade path leading away from Holywood.

carriageway; cross with care and go under a railway bridge to reach the shore of Belfast Lough.

Ulster Way signposts stand on the concrete promenade, where you turn right to start this walk, which is also the North Down Coastal Path. The promenade is equipped with benches, where you could sit and study the Belfast Hills seen across the lough. Follow the path onwards, walking parallel to the railway line at first. Later, the railway veers inland, while you continue across a grassy parkland by the shore.

Pass a small pier and slipway at Cultra Avenue, and continue past the Royal Northern Ireland Yacht Club on Seafront Road. This road continues along the shore as a gravel track, and the 'Private Road' sign applies only to vehicles. Rising for some distance inland is the Ulster Folk and Transport Museum – a vast open-air

INFORMATION

Distance: 10 km (6 miles) as a linear walk.

Start and finish: Start at Holywood, in the centre of town, and finish at Helen's Bay, where trains or buses can be used to return to Holywood.

Terrain: Easy coastal walking. Most of the coastal path has been surfaced, or runs along minor roads. Shoes might be sufficient, but boots would be better in wet weather.

Public transport: Northern Ireland Railway services reach both Holywood and Helen's Bay between Belfast and Bangor. Ulsterbus services 1 and 2 reach Holywood, while Ulsterbus Busybus service 301C links Helen's Bay and Holywood.

Time: Allow up to 4 hours, or longer if you prefer to watch birds along the coast.

Refreshments: There are plenty of places to eat and drink in Holywood, but Helen's Bay has only limited facilities.

Opening hours: *Ulster Folk & Transport Museum, Cultra:* Apr-Jun and Sep, Mon-Fri, 0930–1700, Sat, 1030–1800, Sun, 1200–1800. Jul-Aug, Mon-Sat, 1030–1800, Sun, 1200–1800. Oct-Mar, Mon-Fri, 0930–1600, Sat-Sun, 1230–1630. Admission charge. *Grey Point Fort, Helen's Bay:* Apr-Sep, daily except Tue, 1400–1700. Oct-Mar, Sundays only, 1400–1700. Admission free (01247 853621).

museum displaying many fine buildings which have been rescued from ruin all around the countryside and rebuilt stone by stone at Cultra since the 1950s.

The coast path follows the top of a sea wall for a while, then you pass the end of Glen Road. A concrete path beside garden walls leads to the next narrow shore road. The path continues alongside the tall safety fence bounding a golf course, then runs round a low, rocky, wooded point. If you look out across the lough you could see the Halftide Rock, which might have seals hauled out upon it. It also serves as a perch for cormorants.

The path becomes pleasantly grassy as it continues beside a tall wall. There are areas of shingle and rock before the path passes close to a school and rises gently through an area of scrub and bracken. There is a fork in the path later, where you should keep low and pass the fence of the Seahill Sewage Treatment Works. Seahill could be reached by detouring inland, to link with bus or railway services. The path runs through an arched gateway, then a flight of concrete steps lead uphill over a wooded cliff, and another flight drops back down to the shore again.

A gravelly path by a rocky shore leads into the popular Crawfordsburn Country Park. You pass a boathouse as

The coastal path reaches Crawfordsburn Country Park.

you turn around a small bay, passing the end of a road which leads up into Helen's Bay. Blue waymark arrows on posts indicate the coastal path through the Country Park, but you will hardly need them, as the way ahead is obvious. Follow the path through a turnstile and continue along the top of a low cliff-line on the wooded Grey Point.

A sign indicates a short diversion to the Grey Point Fort – a structure dating from 1904 which was placed here to defend Belfast Lough against possible invasion.

Another promenade path at Helens Bay.

The coastal path continues around Grey Point, and wanders through a wood before reaching another road running through Helen's Bay. By following the road uphill from the beach at Helen's Bay you will reach the railway station, or you could catch a bus back to Holywood.

If you wanted to enjoy a longer walk, you could continue further along the waymarked coastal path and sample some of the other waymarked walks in Crawfordsburn Country Park (Walk 19). Alternatively, you could continue even further, to complete the full length of the North Down Coastal Path to Bangor and Groomsport.

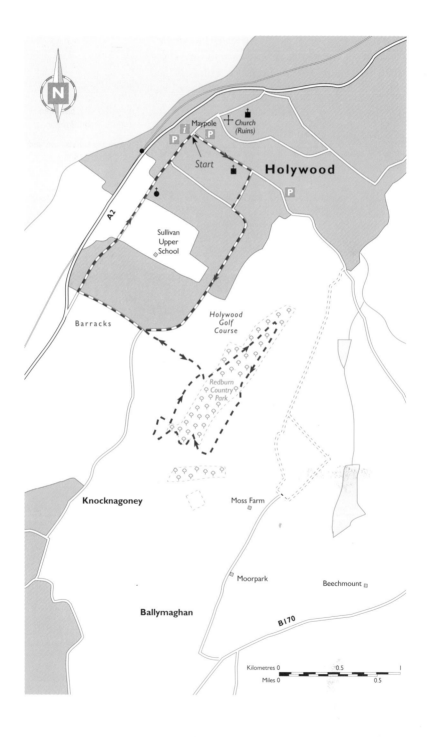

REDBURN COUNTRY PARK

Holywood has a long history, and its name is derived from Sanctus Boscus – Holy Wood. Although the original church of AD 620 is no longer to be seen, the old Priory Church building

in the Priory Graveyard, dating from the 13th century, is worth seeing. Another of Holywood's curiosities is a tall permanent maypole in the centre of town, replacing similar structures which seem to have stood there since the 17th century.

Old church in the Priory Graveyard at Holywood.

Just outside Holywood is Redburn Country Park. This is basically a wooded escarpment facing Belfast Lough which features a network of good paths. The area was once a property of the Dunville family – owners of the famous Dunville Whiskey Company in Belfast. They lived part of the year at Redburn House, the site of which is now occupied by a nursing home. While it is possible to park

alongside Redburn Country Park and enjoy its walks, it is also worth exploring Holywood at the same time, so the walk is structured to run out of town and later back towards it.

View across Holywood from Redburn Country Park.

Start in the centre of Holywood, admiring the tall Maypole at the junction of High Street, Shore Road and Church Street. Follow Church Street uphill to pass the splendid spired Church of Ireland, then turn right along Demesne Road. This road later turns left and

INFORMATION

Distance: 8 km (5 miles).

Start and finish: Holywood, between Belfast and Bangor.

Terrain: Roads in and around Holywood, plus firm, dry paths in the wooded Redburn Country Park. Shoes are normally fine, but wear boots in wet weather.

Public transport: Ulsterbus services 1 and 2 reach Holywood from Bangor or Belfast.

Time: Allow around 2½ hours to explore both Holywood and Redburn Country Park.

Refreshments: Plenty of places to eat and drink around Holywood.

Opening hours: *Redburn Country Park:* always open. Admission free (01247 811491).

right, before continuing to pass Holywood Golf Course. When the road runs downhill, look out on the left for an entrance to Redburn Country Park (2 km from the start).

Tree at sunset in Redburn Country Park.

There is a track running uphill into Redburn Country Park, known as Ardtullagh Avenue. As you climb, the track bends to the right, then at a junction of paths you turn sharply left. The path passes a small quarry known as the Bear Pit. This is a reminder that one of the Dunville family kept a pet bear, as well as an extensive menagerie of other exotic animals.

The path you are following crosses a small cutting called The Ravine, then continues along an undulating course through the delightful Nuns Wood. You may glimpse the golf course and parts of Holywood through the trees. Later, the path climbs more steeply, and by keeping right you will soon be walking along the upper edge of the wooded escarpment. The path reaches The Ravine again, at a higher level, and you cross over it to join a short stretch of the Ulster Way.

Stay high on a path which has the young trees of the New Plantation to the left and a slope of gorse bushes to the right. There are views across Holywood and Belfast Lough to Belfast and the Belfast Hills. Later, the path turns right to run downhill, and you should follow the arrows on the waymark posts which indicate the course of the Ulster Way.

When you cross a footbridge over the stream in Rory's Glen, you will be drawn through an area of rhododendron bushes. In 600 m, look out for a right turn, and follow a path to a car park near the Holywood Private Nursing Home. This was once the site of Redburn House. Follow a path running alongside a fence just above the nursing home. This path twists and turns uphill for about 400 m, and if you then turn left you will be led back downhill a short way.

In 50 m, look out for a turning to the right as you walk downhill and follow a clear gravel path straight onwards. Do not be dismayed when this path appears to dwindle away to nothing, as in 400 m you will suddenly emerge onto a clearer track. This is Ardtullagh Avenue, which was used earlier in the walk, and by turning left and following it downhill you will be led out of Redburn Country Park.

Follow Jackson Road downhill and you will pass alongside the Palace Barracks and an area of Army housing before turning right along Belfast Road. This return route allows you to see a bit more of Holywood. The Roman Catholic church features an old tower connected to a striking new conical church building. Further along, the Presbyterian Church has an impressive and colourful facade. If you continue straight past the Maypole, you will reach the Priory Graveyard, which contains the old Priory Church ruin. Food and drink is of course available throughout the centre of Holywood.

If you wanted to extend the walk, you could set off along a stretch of the North Down Coastal Path, possibly following it as far as Cultra, then taking the rest of the day to explore the Ulster Folk and Transport Museum. Following the Ulster Way from Redburn Country Park towards Belfast is less satisfying, as there is a fair amount of road walking.

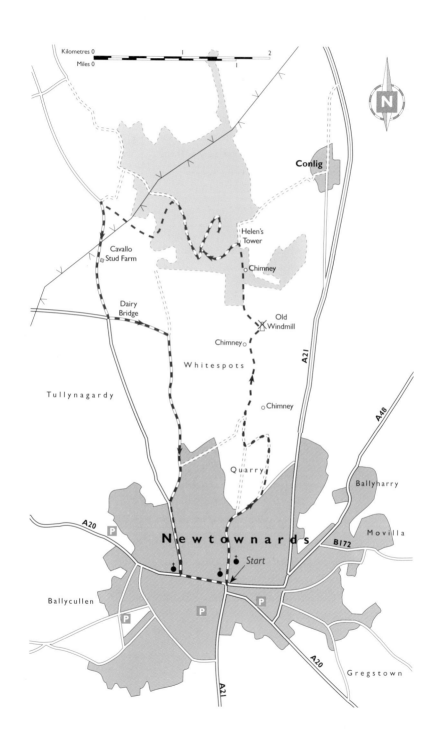

Kilometres 0   1   2

Miles 0   1

N

Conlig

Helen's
Tower

○ Chimney

Cavallo
Stud Farm

Dairy
Bridge

Old
Windmill

Chimney ○

Whitespots

A21

Tullynagardy

○ Chimney

A48

Quarry

Ballyharry

A20   P

Newtownards

Movilla

B172

Start

Ballycullen

P

P

P

A20

A21

Gregstown

WHITESPOTS AND HELEN'S TOWER

Newtownards is the 'new town' on the Ards peninsula; a busy place with plenty of facilities, making a good place to start and finish this walk to Helen's Tower. The walk uses a stretch of the Ulster Way running northwards from Newtownards to Crawfordsburn. You could, if you wanted, go all that way, but this walk is taken as far as Helen's Tower on a wooded brow before returning to Newtownards. The route passes Whitespots, where there is plenty of evidence of mining, as well as a rarity in Ireland – a ruined windmill stump.

There are plenty of places to park around Newtownards, and if you head for the centre of town you can't miss finding the Town Hall. Its well-dressed stone frontage faces the wide, open Conway Square. To start the walk, however, you go round the back of the Town Hall, which is rather shabbier, and follow North Street which runs, predictably, northwards. This is the course of the Ulster Way, though it is some time before you find any waymarks.

Simply follow the main road uphill as if leaving town, and pass the entrance to a works depot. This depot is in an old quarry, and you follow its boundary fence uphill as you continue along the road. Watch for a turning to the left later, where you pass a small compound full of hire cars. You follow a track which is

Old mine chimney above Whitespots.

flanked by hedgerows, then suddenly you have a view into the old quarry as you approach its head.

Turn left to follow a track along the boundary fence at the top edge of the quarry. There are views along the length of Strangford Lough, as well as towards Scrabo Tower and the Mountains of Mourne. When you reach the next corner of the boundary fence, turn right and follow another clear track running gently uphill. There are gates to go through as you continue the gradual ascent through fields.

Away to your right is a tall, old chimney standing in the fields, but you don't go near it. Instead, you follow the track out across the scrub-covered higher ground and aim straight towards another tall chimney. These mark the site of old lead smelting mills. Although the surrounding area has been extensively rutted by motorbike scramblers, you needn't be confused by the network of tracks. Simply walk towards the prominent derelict windmill stump further away.

The idea is to keep heading in roughly the same direction, so that you follow a clear track past a small pond, then pass a gateway into a wood, and walk within sight of a golf course to pass another tall chimney at the edge of the wood. By now, you should have noticed the waymark posts of the Ulster Way,

Helen's Tower rises from a wooded hilltop.

and you follow the arrow markers faithfully through the wood.

The Ulster Way makes a sudden turn to the left, and when you later reach a prominent crossroads of tracks, you have a choice to make. You can either head straight on, following the Ulster Way downhill, or turn right and follow another track to the top of the hill to see Helen's Tower. The tower is a splendid structure, completed in 1850 in honour of Helen, Lady Dufferin. If you visit the tower, be sure to retrace your steps to the Ulster Way afterwards.

Charming small lake passed on the descent.

Follow the Ulster Way downhill through the woods and turn left at another prominent crosstracks. The track you then follow crosses an embankment between two small ponds, where the scenery is charming and there may be waterfowl to observe. Shortly afterwards, the Ulster Way leaves the forest and follows a track to join a rather busy road close to the entrance to a sawmill.

Turn left to follow the road back towards Newtownards, and take care to walk facing the traffic as there is no pavement. You follow this busy road for about 1 km. Walk past the entrance to Cavallo Farm – which is a stud – and turn left at Dairy Bridge to follow the Mountain Road. This is narrow and quiet, passing a number of small farms before reaching the suburbs of Newtownards. Walk straight downhill into town, and finally turn left along the main street to return to the Town Hall. You will pass the bus station on the way, and there are plenty of shops, pubs and restaurants if you need them.

It is possible to extend this walk using the course of the Ulster Way. If you continue beyond Helen's Tower you will pass Clandeboye Estate on the way to Crawfordsburn Country Park. If you head out of Newtownards following the Ulster Way in the other direction, you will quickly gain the slopes of Scrabo Hill crowned by its prominent tower.

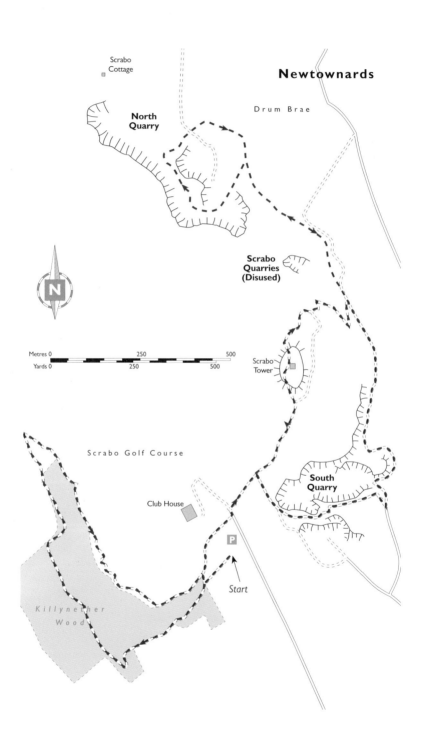

Scrabo
Cottage

Newtownards

Drum Brae

**North
Quarry**

**Scrabo
Quarries
(Disused)**

N

Metres 0   250   500
Yards 0   250   500

Scrabo
Tower

Scrabo Golf Course

**South
Quarry**

Club House

P

Start

*Killynether
Wood*

SCRABO HILL

I t was in 1683 that William Montgomery wrote of 'the high hill called Scrabo . . . ye stones whereof are well known in Dublin, and taken thither and elsewhere in great abundance'. Although most of Scrabo Hill is made of sandstone, the sandstone contains intrusive dykes of dolerite, which gives the hill a hard top and makes it an outstanding feature in an otherwise low, rolling landscape.

There are three short circular walks around Scrabo Country Park, which can be linked together by following the course of the Ulster Way around Scrabo Hill. Cars can be driven up the slopes of Scrabo Hill and parked quite close to Scrabo Tower, but if you arrive using Ulsterbus services to Newtownards, then you can walk towards the hill in a matter of minutes from the town centre.

There are three parts to this short walk. First, a circuit of Killynether Wood, which is a fine beechwood on a steep slope. Second, a climb to the prominent landmark of Scrabo Tower on top of Scrabo Hill. Third, a walk through some old quarries which are gradually being reclaimed by nature.

To reach the start of this walk by car, follow signs for Scrabo Country Park from either Newtownards or Comber. There are two car parks, and you should use the higher one, which is close to Scrabo Golf Course. Scrabo Tower can be seen above the car park, while Killynether Wood is off to the

Scrabo Tower crowns Scrabo Hill.

left as you arrive. There are interpretative noticeboards which you may want to study before starting the walk.

Leave the lower part of the upper car park by following a path into Killynether Wood. The path runs downhill, close to the edge of the beechwood. When you reach the lower car park, turn right to start

Killynether Wood on the slopes of Scrabo Hill.

climbing gradually uphill again. You should notice the waymark posts and arrows which indicate the course of the Ulster Way. Simply follow the clear path uphill, bearing to the right later to traverse along the top side of the wood, returning finally to the upper car park.

Leave the car park by following the clear track straight towards Scrabo Tower, and enjoy the fine views of the surrounding countryside. In clear weather, you can see along the length of Strangford Lough to the Mountains of Mourne. Belfast and the Belfast Hills are also in view, while in very clear conditions, views extend all the way to Galloway in Scotland. Scrabo Tower is properly called the Londonderry Monument, and was built in memory of the 3rd Marquis of Londonderry, Charles William Stewart. On occasions

A view across
Newtownards from
Scrabo Hill.

the building, which dates from the 1850s, is open to
visitors, so that you can enjoy a more extensive view
from an even higher elevation.

To leave Scrabo Tower, follow a less well defined path
more steeply downhill towards Newtownards. The
path passes through scrub before zig-zagging down the
wooded slopes. When you land on a broad, gravel
path, turn left and follow it as it contours along the
side of the hill. Further along, there is a turning off to
the left, where the path passes through a sheer-sided
rock cutting to enter an old quarry. This is the North
Quarry, which is delightfully overgrown, but must
have been something of an eyesore in its heyday.

Follow the path through the North Quarry, reaching a
point where four paths meet, and gradually bear to the
right along clear paths until you pass the point where
you earlier turned into North Quarry through the
cutting. Go straight along the path this time, retracing
some of your earlier steps and passing beneath Scrabo
Tower, to reach the South Quarry.

As you pass the quarry, you also pass a low barrier gate,
then turn right to go up a flight of steps so that you can
overlook the South Quarry. From a vantage point
beside an informative notice board, you can see the
greenish bands of dolerite running through the lighter
sandstone. Continue along the path to return to the
car park where you started the walk. In a field
alongside the car park you might notice a series of
white stones set into the ground to represent the bones
of a dinosaur!

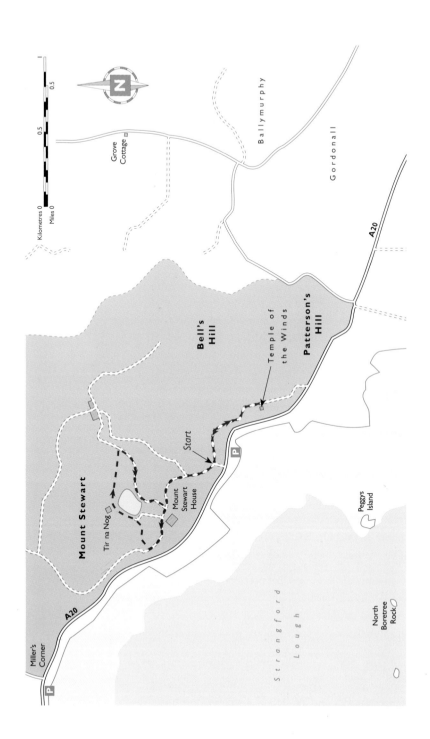

MOUNT STEWART

Mount Stewart is a National Trust property on the shore of Strangford Lough between Newtownards and Greyabbey. At the centre of the estate is a fine house, surrounded by beautiful and varied ornamental gardens and further enhanced by delightful mixed woodlands.

View from the Lake Walk at Mount Stewart.

The walk is quite short and could be quickly completed, but there is so much to see that you could spend several hours exploring Mount Stewart. The only thing to note is that the property will almost certainly be closed during the winter months, and there is an entry charge to be paid to see the house and gardens, unless you are a National Trust member. The car park is located a short way along the access road from the entrance gates, and Ulsterbus services pass the gates.

Drive or walk along the access road from the entrance gates, and obtain your ticket to visit the gardens. You can also buy a booklet containing a detailed map of the grounds. There are formal gardens close to Mount Stewart House, and you can please yourself how long and in what manner you explore them. The celebrated gardens were designed by Edith, Lady Londonderry, and contain unusual sculptures as well as many rare plants. The colonnaded frontage of the house makes a fine backdrop to the beautiful surroundings.

INFORMATION

Distance: 4 km (2.5 miles).

Start and finish: At the car park close to Mount Stewart House, between Newtownards and Greyabbey.

Terrain: Firm and dry paths and tracks through gardens and woodlands. No special footwear necessary.

Public transport: Ulsterbus services 9 and 10 reach Mount Stewart, but check the timetable as not every bus passes the entrance gates.

Time: Allow around 2 hours for the walk, or longer to explore the house and ornamental gardens in detail.

Refreshments: There is a shop and tea room at Mount Stewart, and if these are closed, you can find food and drink not too far away at Greyabbey.

Opening hours:
Mount Stewart Gardens: Apr-Sep, daily, 1030–1800. Oct, Sat-Sun only, 1030–1800. *Mount Stewart House and Temple of the Winds:* May-Sep, daily except Tue, 1300–1800, Apr and Oct, Sat-Sun only, 1300–1800. Admission charge for house and gardens (012477 88387/88487).

Tir na Nog-the Land of
Eternal Youth.

To explore the grounds further, follow the broad tarmac track beyond Mount Stewart House, passing a variety of trees and shrubs. Watch carefully on the right for a small sign indicating the start of the Lake View Walk. This little woodland path climbs gently uphill a short way and overlooks an ornamental lake which is fringed with a variety of fine trees and plants.

The path drifts downhill and joins a much clearer path which practically encircles the lake. As you follow the path around the lake, look out for flights of stone steps rising on the left. These lead up to the family burial ground of Tir nan Og – the Land of Eternal Youth. The public are not admitted to the walled ornamental garden, but you can peep through a pair of iron gates and study the interior layout.

Sculpture of a deer at
Mount Stewart.

Walk back down to the path and continue following it, noting that it now begins to drift away from the lake. Away to the left is a sculpture of a deer – painted white, with antlers, and with barbed wire across its back to prevent children climbing all over it! Further along you reach a junction of tracks where you turn right to follow the Ladies Walk back towards Mount Stewart House.

The return is along broad and clear gravel paths, but you also have the option of walking through the Rhododendron Wood off to the left, where you can follow a series of grassy paths between the rhododendron bushes instead. You can either return to the house, or the car park, or enjoy a further short extension to the walk to visit the Temple of the Winds.

To do this, walk back along the access road from the car park towards the entrance gates, then continue along another woodland track running roughly parallel to the main road. This track climbs gently uphill to reach the Temple of the Winds – an octagonal building which crowns a low drumlin above Strangford Lough. Originally built in 1780, the temple has recently been restored.

Follow the track back towards the entrance gates, and if you want to walk briefly beside the shore of Strangford Lough, cross the main road and climb up onto the top of a strange-looking building to look out across the lough. This building is actually an old gasworks, and from the top of it, which has been converted into a bird hide, you can see across the lough to the Mountains of Mourne. The entire foreshore of Strangford Lough is managed as part of a Wildlife Scheme by the National Trust.

Before leaving the Mount Stewart area, anyone with an interest in antiques should make a visit to the nearby village of Greyabbey, which features a ruined Cistercian abbey and a physic garden – and a surprising number of antiques shops for such a small place.

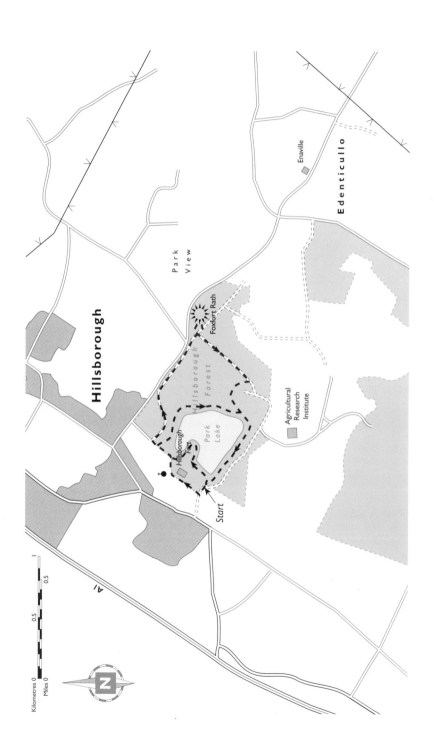

HILLSBOROUGH

alkers who like to study architecture and old buildings will find Hillsborough a remarkable little village. Although it is built on a hillside, the place actually takes its name from Colonel Arthur Hill, who built Hillsborough Fort in 1650. A quick tour of Hillsborough reveals not only the fort, but also a splendid Parish Church with a tall spire and two decorative towers. There is plenty of Georgian architecture, and imposing civic buildings, as well as memorials to various local worthies. A stone tablet at the entrance to the fort tells how the collapse of talks once held there may have been responsible for the start of the American War of Independence.

Hillsborough Forest is found immediately alongside Hillsborough village, and road signs direct motorists to a forest car park. Anyone arriving using Ulsterbus

INFORMATION

Distance: 5 km (3 miles) by combining short waymarked trails.

Start and finish: At the entrance to Hillsborough Forest, off Park Street in Hillsborough.

Terrain: Mostly along level, firm, dry paths and tracks through mixed woodlands and along the lakeshore. Shoes would normally be sufficient, but wear boots in wet weather.

Public transport: Ulsterbus services 38, 200 and 238 pass through Hillsborough between Belfast and Banbridge.

Time: Allow 2 to 2½ hours to walk along all the waymarked trails in Hillsborough Forest.

Refreshments: Places to eat and drink can be found in Hillsborough village, just alongside the forest.

Opening hours: *Hillsborough Fort:* Tue-Sat, 1000–1900. Admission free.

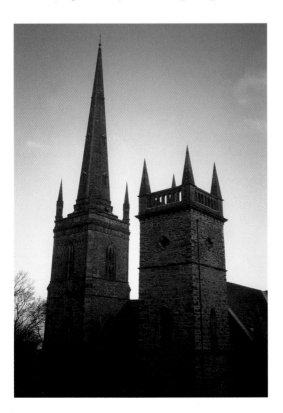

Tower and spire of the Parish Church at Hillsborough

services can easily walk into the forest from the village. There is a charming little lake, delightful mixed woodlands and a network of paths and tracks allowing you to explore it all. The walk offered here is a combination of three waymarked trails. The Foxfort Rath Trail wanders practically all around the perimeter of Hillsborough Forest, while the Lake Trail naturally encircles Hillsborough Lake, and the Castle Trail simply takes a short walk around Hillsborough Fort.

Looking across Hillsborough Lake.

Starting from the forest car park, walk past an information board which outlines the routes of the three trails. Turn left along the top of the dam of Hillsborough Lake to start following the Foxfort Rath Trail, which is marked by red arrows on wooden posts. You walk off the dam, travel around a grassy point in the lake, then head across another dam. Route directions are hardly necessary as the waymarking system is so good – and the trail uses clear paths and tracks.

The Foxfort Rath Trail runs close to the boundary wall of the forest, which was constructed in 1841, and eventually reaches Foxfort Rath, which features the typical earthern ramparts of a rath. Originally, Foxfort Rath would have had a wooden palisade on top of its circular earthern ramparts, and there would have been a handful of wattle buildings inside. The rath would have been occupied by a fairly prosperous extended family and operated basically as a fortified farmstead in early Christian times. It is situated on a loop in the trail, which then continues along a broad track through a younger part of the forest.

The final part of the Foxfort Rath Trail runs concurrent with the Lake Trail, along the wooded shores of Hillsborough Lake, and so is also marked with blue waymark arrows. When you return to the car park, walk down through it and pick up the line of yellow waymark arrows which indicate the route of the Castle Trail. Walk along the service road to reach Hillsborough Fort, which you can explore when its gates are open. The Castle Trail runs between the Fort and the Parish Church, to reach the shores of Hillsborough Lake again.

Hillsborough Fort, around which Hillsborough grew.

You now turn left and cross the dam, and you should realise that you have already crossed this dam earlier while following the Foxfort Rath Trail. This time you turn off right as indicated by the blue arrows of the Lake Trail. A woodland path soon reaches the lake shore, then the path becomes clearer and is seldom out of sight of the water as it makes a complete circuit of the lake.

The Lake Trail crosses a footbridge near a patch of reedmace at the head of the lake, then runs back to the forest car park in the company of the Foxfort Rath Trail, which was also followed earlier. When you have completed all three of the short waymarked trails, don't be in a hurry to leave, but spend an hour or so wandering around Hillsborough village to soak up its history.

Hillsborough Castle can be glimpsed through a pair of magnificent wrought iron gates, and this fine mansion is generally used to entertain any royalty and politicians who visit Northern Ireland. Apart from an outstanding Georgian market house and several typical Georgian townhouses, Hillsborough has some narrow alleyways filled with charming little terraced houses, while antiques and craft shops can be found along the main street.

INDEX

Opposite: Belfast Castle and the prow of Cave Hill.

Other titles in this series

25 Walks – In and Around Aberdeen
25 Walks – Cotswolds
25 Walks – The Chilterns
25 Walks – Deeside
25 Walks – Dumfries and Galloway
25 Walks – Edinburgh and Lothian
25 Walks – Fife
25 Walks – In and Around Glasgow
25 Walks – Highland Perthshire
25 Walks – The Scottish Borders
25 Walks – The Trossachs
25 Walks – The Western Isles
25 Walks – The Yorshire Dales

Other titles in preparation

25 Walks – In Argyll
(Cowall, Arrocher and Bute)
25 Walks – Down
25 Walks – Fermanagh
25 Walks – In and Around London

Long distance guides published by The Stationery Office

The West Highland Way – Official Guide
The Southern Upland Way – Official Guide

The Stationery Office

Published by The Stationery Office and available from:

The Stationery Office Bookshops
71 Lothian Road, Edinburgh EH3 9AZ
(counter service only)
South Gyle Crescent, Edinburgh EH12 9EB
(mail, fax and telephone orders only)
0131-479 3141 Fax 0131-479 3142
49 High Holborn, London WC1V 6HB
(counter service and fax orders only)
Fax 0171-831 1326
68-69 Bull Street, Birmingham B4 6AD
0121-236 9696 Fax 0121-236 9699
33 Wine Street, Bristol BS1 2BQ
0117-926 4306 Fax 0117-929 4515
9-21 Princess Street, Manchester M60 8AS
0161-834 7201 Fax 0161-833 0634
16 Arthur Street, Belfast BT1 4GD
01232 238451 Fax 01232 235401
The Stationery Office Oriel Bookshop
The Friary, Cardiff CF1 4AA
01222 395548 Fax 01222 384347

The Stationery Office publications are also available from:

The Publications Centre
(mail, telephone and fax orders only)
PO Box 276, London SW8 5DT
General enquiries 0171-873 0011
Telephone orders 0171-873 9090
Fax orders 0171-873 8200

Accredited Agents
(see Yellow Pages)

and through good booksellers

Printed in Scotland for The Stationery Office by c.c. No 70343 50c 10/96